DIVORCE
&
CHILD
CUSTODY

Your Options
and Legal Rights

DIVORCE
&
CHILD
CUSTODY

Your Options
and Legal Rights

Deanna Peters
Richard L. Strohm

Chelsea House Publishers

Philadelphia

First published in hardback edition in 1997 by Chelsea House Publishers.

1 3 5 7 9 8 6 4 2

Library of Congress Cataloging-in-Publication Data

Peters, Deanna.
    Layman's law guides. Divorce and child custody / by Deanna Peters and
Richard L. Strohm.
        p. cm.
Rev. ed. of: Divorce and child custody. 2nd ed. c1994.
Includes index.
    ISBN 0-7910-4439-4 (hc)
    1. Divorce—Law and legislation—United States—Popular works.
    2. Custody of children—United States—Popular works. I. Strohm,
Richard L. II. Peters, Deanna. Divorce and child custody.
III. Title.
KF535.Z9P48 1997
346.7301'66—dc21   96-48969
                                                                     CIP

ACKNOWLEGEMENTS

Many thanks to super secretaries Donna Johnson and Sally Murfin. Thanks also to the Honorable Barry G. Silverman, again (such a debt I owe!) and my partners.

But none of this would be possible without the support of Chris "Goose" and Marie, or Dr. Wayne Dyer, who teaches that the highest good always comes from listening to your inner signals. Without Wayne's inspiration, I would still be wondering whether to take on the LawGuides project.

RICHARD L. STROHM

A special thanks to my friend, Judy Nichols, who read and re-read this manuscript and offered many helpful suggestions. Her dedication to helping make this book a success is greatly appreciated. We had a tough time with certain words, but I think we finally got it right!

Appreciation also goes out to two very special people in my office, Michelle Saba and Diane Trevino. As always, they've done a great job managing the office and the daily work-load while I sat for hours in front of my computer, writing and re-writing. Their patience and cooperation are true signs of their loyalty and dedication.

And, many thanks to my husband, Mark, who has supported me and encouraged me through every venture I've undertaken. His patience, encouragement and confidence in me mean more than I could ever express in words.

DEANNA PETERS

TABLE OF CONTENTS ....

HOW TO USE THIS PUBLICATION ....

This publication is designed to provide the reader with information relating to domestic relations laws. This book provides information on marriage, divorce, child custody and other family law matters, and is written to provide you with basic information. Not everything in this book will apply to you, because not every set of circumstances is the same.

While this publication is designed to help you understand the general laws of domestic relations, remember that divorce and custody are matters of state law. One uniform law of divorce and custody does not exist; rather fifty separate laws apply—one for each state. To make matters even more complicated, each state has its own court procedures and rules for obtaining a divorce. But, don't be discouraged. There are certain basic concepts which apply most everywhere, and we have explained them in simple terms so that you can evaluate your position and understand your legal rights.

Sometimes people are overwhelmed with the thought of divorce. If they cannot afford to hire a lawyer they may continue in the marriage and hope things will get better, only to realize they usually don't. It is important that you know what the law is with regard to domestic matters. People who know how the law works are better able to plan their best course of action. Don't be influenced by anyone else's claims about what they think the law states; find out for yourself.

This book does not go into detail regarding contested divorce matters or the various forms of discovery (a legal term referring to the process of finding out about the other person's case) which may apply in a contested divorce. If you expect your divorce to be contested and/or if your spouse retains a lawyer, then you also should consult a lawyer—DO NOT represent yourself under such circumstances.

How can this book help? We hope it will explain the concepts, define the terms, and help you unravel the complexities of the domestic relations laws. It also will guide you through the divorce process, step-by-step, and provide an overview of how to handle your own uncontested no fault, default divorce.

CHAPTER ONE
MARRIAGE AND DIVORCE
. . . .

What Is Marriage?

Marriage is a legal status which is created either by a formal ceremony or by living together in states which recognize common law marriages. A valid marriage requires the consent of two adult persons of the opposite sex who are not prohibited from marriage because of a family relationship. There are serious legal, financial and moral consequences to marriage which create rights and duties enforceable by the laws of your state.

To ensure that a marriage is legal, a couple must first obtain a marriage license or certificate from the clerk of the court. Most states require that the parties apply in person for the marriage license and supply the necessary information on the application under oath. A nominal fee is charged for the marriage license. A marriage ceremony must be performed by a person authorized by law, such as a licensed or ordained clergyman, judge or justice of the peace. The ceremony usually must be performed in the presence of one or two adult witnesses, depending on your state, and the officiating officer. The marriage license or certificate must then be signed by the parties and witnesses, and recorded after the ceremony with the county recorder's office.

> *Marriage is a legal status which is created either by a formal ceremony or by living together in a state which recognizes common law marriages.*

In the past, it was custom for the wife to take the surname of her husband; however this is not always the case today. Many women prefer to retain their maiden name even after marriage. Whether the wife chooses to take the name of her husband or retain her own surname makes no difference, as the law does not require a woman to take her husband's surname.

Every state has its own laws regarding the rights and duties of married persons. When a marriage complies with the formalities imposed in the state where the ceremony took place, the marriage is considered valid everywhere. In other words, so long as the marriage is valid in the state or country where it took place, the marriage will be considered valid in your state, even if your state has different requirements to marry.

Duties of Spouses

Each spouse has an equal obligation to provide financial support for the necessities of life.

Each spouse is expected to contribute to the well-being of the other and an equal obligation exists to provide financial support for the necessities of life. In previous years, it was presumed that the husband was the income earner and the wife the homemaker. This presumption no longer exists today. The law now views each party as an equal. In the event of divorce, it is possible for a husband to receive spousal maintenance, just as it has been possible in the past for a wife to receive spousal maintenance.

Basically, whether a court will or will not order financial support after divorce is based upon a variety of factors. The court presumes that each party in a marriage is capable of providing for himself after the marriage is dissolved, but sometimes that isn't the case and a judge will take the matter into consideration. For example, a judge is likely to order spousal maintenance to be paid to an invalid spouse by a healthy one. Additionally, in deciding how to divide property after a marriage, the courts will often consider the needs of each party.

Whether it is the husband or the wife who is working, or both, the courts try to divide the property in such a way that the obligations and responsibilities are equal, assuming that each spouse has equal means to pay for the liabilities. In cases where one spouse has more education, business experience or income, this may not be possible.

Parental Duties

Both parents owe duties of support, love and affection to their children unless the parental rights have been terminated by a court order. This is true even if the parents were never married or are divorced. The duties of both parents are equal. The idea that it is the mother's sole responsibility to care for the children is not recognized by the law. Both parents must provide financial support for their children or they can be taken to court and forced to pay.

Both parents must provide financial support for their children or they can be taken to court and forced to pay.

Domestic Torts: Suing Your Spouse for Damages

A *tort* is a legal term which means a civil wrong. Auto accidents, slip and fall accidents and malpractice claims are examples of tort suits. In essence, somebody is demanding money, or damages, for a wrong done to them. The law is changing and the trend in the law is to allow these types of suits between spouses. These kinds of claims for tort suits between spouses usually are based on assault and battery; intentional or negligent infliction of emotional harm;

false imprisonment; defamation or libel (slander is oral defamation whereas libel is written defamation); fraudulent conversion, concealment or transfer of marital assets; and kidnapping of the children.

Whether the courts and juries grant damages depends upon the law of your particular state. You must consult with a lawyer to determine whether you have a claim against your spouse for damages, according to your state's laws. It is important to contact a lawyer regarding domestic torts because some states require you to combine claims for tort damages with claims you may have in your divorce proceeding. For example, Alabama, Georgia, Nevada, New Jersey, New York, Texas and Tennessee require a combination of tort claims with the petition for divorce. If you do not combine a tort claim with the divorce filing, you may forfeit the claim.

Other states have just the opposite rule and if you combine a tort claim against your spouse with your divorce petition, you may be thrown out of court. In Arizona, Colorado, Indiana, Iowa, Massachusetts, New Hampshire, Utah and Wisconsin, you should not combine a tort claim with your divorce petition.

If you think you may have a suit for damages, carefully review the facts with a lawyer.

The point is, you should be aware that you may be entitled to damages depending upon your state's law. Carefully review the facts of your particular case with a lawyer. Even if you plan to handle your own divorce, consult a lawyer who specializes in personal injury suits to help you with the tort claim. If you are using a lawyer in your divorce, be sure to disclose the facts which may constitute a tort to your lawyer so he can take the appropriate steps to protect your interests.

If you think you may have a suit for damages against your spouse, you should find that it is easy to obtain legal representation. Lawyers usually charge by the hour or sometimes on a flat fee basis for domestic cases such as divorce, custody, etc. A lawyer's ethical code and some state statutes specifically prohibit a lawyer from taking a divorce or custody matter on a contingency fee basis. A contingency fee arrangement is one where the lawyer receives no payment for his fees unless there is a recovery. In all contingency cases, the costs of the suit such as deposition costs, witness fees and court costs still remain the responsibility of the client whether the case is won or lost.

A contingency fee arrangement is one where the lawyer receives no payment unless there is a recovery.

Most lawyers who accept cases involving tort claims take them on a contingency fee basis. In a case where you think you may have a claim against your spouse for intentional infliction of emotional distress, for example, a lawyer may take the case on a one-third contingency basis. In other words, he will take one-third of the total amount of money recovered; however, he will not be paid if he is unsuccessful. Contingency fees are negotiable, and sometimes a lawyer will ask for a larger percentage if he feels the case is more difficult to prove, or he may take a lower percentage fee if he feels the case is easy to prove, or if you request that he accept a lesser fee. Don't forget that in every contingency fee case, as in every other kind of case, there will be court costs. Although your lawyer may pay for certain costs up front, you will still be responsible for reimbursing him for costs incurred whether you win

5

or lose your case. Be sure to discuss the estimated amount of the costs of litigation with your lawyer at the outset of your case.

One of the most rapidly developing areas of the law involves domestic torts where one spouse claims that the other spouse has intentionally inflicted emotional harm. How can it be, you may wonder, that one state will allow such actions while another state will not? Differences occur because each state is free to interpret the social policy of that state. That means legislators, judges and lawyers from different states do not necessarily agree about whether it is a good idea to allow spouses to sue each other. The controversy comes down to this: those opposed to allowing individuals to recover damages against their spouses for domestic torts argue that these lawsuits create yet another weapon for one spouse to use against the other while they are separating.

It encourages the filing of cases which may not have a good basis in fact as a means of gaining leverage over the spouse who is sued (i.e. "Give me the house in the divorce proceeding and I won't file a tort claim against you"). Opponents also argue that these kinds of cases create long and drawn out proceedings that the no fault divorce proceeding was designed to stop. In addition, they argue that these kinds of cases force the law to set standards of reasonable conduct for spouses within a marriage. This opens a can of worms about what each person's duty is to the other while they are married.

The argument in favor of allowing such damage suits between spouses focuses on the premise that just because two people are married, it does not mean one can avoid paying for the physical

Domestic tort suits are one of the most rapidly developing areas of law.

or emotional harm inflicted upon the other. In other words, being married or being a parent should not give a person special immunity for abuse or wrongs that a person could get damages for if the abuse or wrongs were inflicted by a stranger instead of a spouse. The trend toward allowing tort suits across the country is likely to continue.

In the old days, the law treated women and children as the possessions of the husband or father. The husband or father's acts were privileged and there was immunity for the husband or father for most wrongs that he committed against his wife or children. Slowly this has changed. So called "inter-spousal immunity" has ended in the United States. Even so, the law does not automatically recognize suits for damages against a spouse. These suits are decided on not only a state by state basis but on a case by case basis.

In the old days, the law treated women and children as possessions of the husband.

As of the writing of this book, only eight states specifically recognize intentional infliction of emotional distress against a spouse as a tort for damages allowable under the state law. They are Colorado, Iowa, Maryland, New Mexico, Oregon, Texas, Utah and Wisconsin.

Please keep in mind that the claim of intentional infliction of emotional harm requires that you prove extreme or outrageous conduct by the wrongdoing spouse along with injury and causation before you can get damages. In other words, the usual stress associated with the break up of a marriage is not sufficient to be awarded money damages.

Finally, intentional infliction of emotional harm is only one of many possible tort claims which could be brought against a spouse as noted earlier in this section. As the law changes, so do your rights and responsibilities. For more information, contact the American Bar Association's Family Law Section, at 750 N. Lake Shore Drive, Chicago, IL 60611, for a copy of the book, *Marital and Parental Torts: A Guide to Causes of Action, Arguments and Damages.* Please remember that this ABA book is written for lawyers.

Domestic Violence

Often it is difficult to take action in a situation of domestic violence. For a variety of reasons, victims of domestic violence may find it difficult to take the steps necessary to address their situation. Even so, domestic violence is not something which should be ignored.

In every state it is illegal for one spouse to cause bodily harm or to abuse the other spouse.

In every state it is illegal for one spouse to cause bodily harm or to abuse the other spouse. What constitutes abuse is defined by your state's written laws known as statutes. Abuse usually involves physical harm. Your state's criminal code will determine whether a prosecutor can file criminal charges against your spouse. If the prosecutor believes that a case can be proven, he will file charges against your spouse, provided that you agree to cooperate by testifying. Most prosecutors' offices have social workers or counselors who can help you. We strongly urge you to contact your local county, district or state prosecutor if you have been abused.

Whether or not you prosecute in court, always get away from the abuser immediately.

The fact that you leave your home to avoid further abuse cannot be used as a reason not to allow you to move back in after the situation has been resolved. Some people stay in an abusive relationship because they are afraid that if they leave they will not be able to get spousal maintenance or child support. Some think they'll lose their rights to their home. These assumptions are false. The law does not require you or your children to suffer at the hands of an abusive spouse in order to maintain any future claims of support or property. The fact that you left your spouse in order to protect yourself or for your child's safety is not grounds to deny support or refuse to award you certain property, assuming that you are otherwise entitled to it.

You need not suffer at the hands of an abusive spouse in order to maintain future claims of support.

If you have nowhere to turn, there are battered women's shelters in most every city which can help you get protection from your spouse. Most shelters also provide counseling services or they can refer you to counseling services which can help you. Information regarding these types of shelters can be obtained from the police department, marriage counselors, crisis intervention centers or the telephone directory.

Many states have domestic violence laws in addition to criminal laws which provide civil penalties for abuse. For instance, a violation of a civil violence statute often carries with it the power of the court to order the abuser to leave the home, refrain from contacting you or the children and require the abuser to pay bills associated with the abuse. Other remedies also may be available to the victim of abuse.

If you find yourself the victim of abuse, it is important to make a record of the abuse as soon as possible by calling the police immediately. While the police usually don't want to get involved in your dispute, they are obligated by law to keep the peace. You may use the police to prevent further harm to you and your children while you gather your belongings so that you can peacefully leave your home. In some states the police officer has the authority to remove the abuser from the home.

If you find yourself the victim of abuse, call the police immediately.

You must consider whether to prosecute criminally or bring a civil action against your spouse by requesting a restraining order preventing him from contacting you or coming near you. When children are involved this sometimes creates complications. An abused spouse may feel that bringing a civil or criminal action will result in more abuse. Discuss the facts of your situation with your county or district attorney's office. Even if you don't prosecute your spouse criminally, the lawyers on staff may be able to refer you to another agency which may be able to help you.

Next, you should obtain any medical treatment necessary. Make sure you get the name of the emergency room physician, since he may be an important witness in your case if you go to court. If possible, have photographs taken as evidence of the abuse. Do not move back in or allow an abuser to move back in until you are satisfied that the abuser is no longer a threat. It is a good idea to obtain counseling before you continue to live together with an abusive spouse.

Most states have a simplified procedure to obtain an immediate order of protection against a violent spouse. Some courts provide the forms for an order of protection, and the filing fee to start the process is nominal. If you want legal protection from the abuser, usually you must go to court. You may be required to appear before a judge and explain the events giving rise to the order of protection. If the judge signs the order, any future violation of an order could result in the offender's arrest and incarceration.

Once papers are served on the abusive spouse, an order of protection restricts the spouse from coming near the abused spouse's home, place of employment, school or any other specified location. Further, it prohibits the spouse from engaging in unlawful violent acts. The court has the power to order that the abuser stay away and be restrained from committing any further acts of violence against you. The advantage of having this order is that the police will be required to enforce it. In situations where there is no order, the police usually are reluctant to get involved. When an order has been obtained, an abuser who violates the order will be physically removed by the police and usually put in jail pending a contempt hearing.

If you are a battered spouse, don't hesitate to contact the court clerk for the procedures to obtain an order of protection. If your spouse violates the order, call the police immediately and have him arrested.

If you are a battered spouse, do not hesitate to obtain an order of protection.

It is important that you make a decision as to whether you believe your marriage is worth saving in view of the abuse. If you are unsure about your marriage, consider seeing a trained counselor who will be objective about your circumstances and problems. This is not to say that discussing the matter with your family is unimportant, but keep in mind that your family knows you and your spouse and usually family members have opinions which may be biased, prejudiced or not objective. Always speak to a trained professional who will be impartial. In the event you decide to stay in the marriage, you should insist that your spouse receive counseling with you on a regular basis. It is unrealistic to believe that an abuser will change over night or without professional counseling. For your own physical safety and for the safety of your children, you both should receive counseling if you decide to stay together and work things out.

Any sort of physical abuse is adequate grounds in any state for a divorce.

Any sort of physical abuse is adequate grounds in any state for a divorce. If you have been a victim of abuse and believe your marriage is not worth saving, do not hesitate to proceed with filing for divorce. Don't make a decision to stay with an abuser simply because you are afraid that you will lose assets of the marriage—your children, your retirement, your home. The courts will generally be sympathetic to the victim. Although it is not as common, husbands also can be the victims of domestic violence. The same remedies explained above apply to husbands who have suffered from domestic violence. With respect to child abuse, most states have proceedings involving the removal of abused children from the environment where the abuse takes place. This includes taking away the rights of parents to have custody of their children, as well as the imposition of court orders preventing the parents from doing certain things.

Getting Help

For help with spousal abuse, contact your state or county prosecutor's office, or check in the telephone directory under State Government. For more information, contact:

National Domestic Violence Hotline
(800) 333-SAFE

National Coalition Against Domestic Violence
P.O. Box 34103 Washington, DC 20043-41033; (202) 638-6388 or (202) 638-6389

National Organization for Women (N.O.W.)
Legal Defense and Education Fund
99 Hudson Street New York, NY 10013
(212) 925-6635

National Organization for Victim Assistance
1757 Park Road, NW Washington, DC 20010; (202) 232-6682

National Center on Child Abuse and Neglect
Department of Health & Human Services
P.O. Box 1182 Washington, DC 20013
(202) 245-0586

The book, *State by State Guide to Women's Legal Rights*, also is a good source of information. It's available from book stores and sells for $12.95.

What is Divorce?

Divorce is a formal court proceeding ending the marital rights and responsibilities of each party. It is important to remember that each state follows its own laws, and each state has slightly different procedures in processing a divorce. Also remember the divorce process is really a lawsuit and therefore, it is a formal court proceeding. Contested divorces often are more painful and time consuming than uncontested matters, which often are relatively quick and inexpensive. Although we don't think of divorce in the traditional way that we think of lawsuits, both contested and uncontested divorces are still governed by your court's rules of civil procedure.

State laws governing when a court can grant a divorce have changed tremendously in the past few years, and continue to change today. The old English law, before the time of Henry VIII, prohibited divorces. In those days, a marriage lasted forever unless it was annulled. Henry VIII was the first exception to the law. Beginning with him, the English courts first recognized divorce as legal, but only for him! As time passed, divorce slowly became a possibility for others. As divorce became more popular, the legal grounds, or reasons why a court could legally grant a divorce gradually expanded. In fact, most states now have some sort of no fault divorce. No fault means the court will order a divorce if both spouses agree that the marriage should end, and neither party alleges fault by the other party.

The idea behind no fault divorce is that couples, not the law, should decide whether or not to continue their marriage.

Remember though, that the states started out by recognizing only those grounds which the old English laws recognized. These grounds were things like adultery, insanity or the inability to procreate. Before no fault divorce, spouses had to fit within one of the state's recognized grounds or they couldn't get divorced. The idea behind no fault divorce is that couples, not the law, should decide whether or not to continue their marriage. If they don't want to continue the marital relationship, why should the law force them to stay together? Or worse, force them to try to fit their case within one of the recognized grounds for divorce. The no fault system recognized that it's worse to force people to claim adultery, even if it's not true, just so they can be free of each other. The people who opposed no fault felt that allowing no fault divorce made it too easy to avoid responsibilities and would contribute to the breakdown of the family. However, the no fault system is here to stay, basically as a result of compromise: no fault is allowed, but judges still decide the issues of what the ex-spouses' rights and responsibilities are after they decide to end the marriage, based on the laws regarding property in each state.

Grounds are the legal reasons, which vary with state laws, upon which the court may order the marriage to be dissolved. In most states, the judge cannot consider the wrongs committed by one spouse when trying to figure out how to divide the property. Generally, the fight between spouses is not over the grounds for divorce but who gets what and who pays for what.

"Grounds" are the legal reasons upon which the court may order the marriage to be dissolved.

The terms, Decree of Dissolution of Marriage or Dissolution Order or Dissolution Judgment mean the same thing. Each is the formal order the judge signs which legally ends the marriage. They usually have a property settlement agreement attached as well. The Property Settlement Agreement distributes the couple's assets and requires each person to pay certain bills or other obligations. If there are children common to the marriage, another document is also signed by the court, usually called a Child Support Order. The order will state the amount of child support to be paid and when the support obligation begins. Usually, support starts upon the entry of the final divorce decree, unless it was previously ordered by the court.

Remember that the judge is going to do three things in your divorce: (1) end the marriage; (2) order the assets to be divided between the parties; and (3) order the parties to pay the debts and liabilities incurred during the marriage. If you have requested spousal maintenance and you have children, the judge also will (1) consider ordering spousal maintenance in a just and fair amount; (2) award custody of the children to either parent or both of you (with reasonable visitation for the non-custodial parent); and (3) order that child support be paid to the custodial parent.

Why Divorce is Legally Necessary

If you determine that your marriage is beyond repair, it is wise to file for divorce as soon as possible.

Once married according to the law of the state or the country where the marriage took place, certain rights and duties automatically govern your role as a spouse. The obligations of the marriage cannot be transferred, assigned or ended except by court order or death. By marrying, you enter into a world full of obligations and responsibilities which you did not have before you married. If you determine that your marriage is beyond repair, it is wise to file for divorce as soon as possible. Many people move out and do nothing to end the marriage. This can create serious difficulties including the inability to locate the spouse in order to serve legal papers.

Remember, even if you and your spouse agree to end the marriage, it is not enough just to live separately. A court order is still required to formally dissolve the relationship, and set forth the responsibilities of each individual after the marriage has ended. If you do not get a court order dissolving the marriage and your spouse goes his separate way and runs up credit card debt or hurts someone, you may still be legally liable for his actions. If you have a court order ending the marriage, you cannot be held liable for anything your ex-spouse does after the date the judge signs the order dissolving your marriage.

Don't make the mistake of moving out and starting a new life separate from your spouse, without first starting the divorce process. People wonder why the courts should tell them what to do with their love life. The answer is that the law establishes an orderly way of ending the responsibilities and rights created by the marriage in a manner that is supposed to be fair to all concerned. This extends to the parties themselves, their children, their creditors and others.

Similar reasoning applies in the case where children are involved. Since minor children aren't self sufficient, the law imposes a special burden on the courts to see to it that the children are treated fairly during a divorce. After all, the children are totally innocent and dependent upon their parents. All too often, the children become pawns of jealous and angry parents. The law recognizes this, and therefore requires judges to protect them during divorce proceedings.

The law imposes a special burden on the courts to see to it that children are treated fairly during a divorce.

Ending a Marital Relationship According to the Law

There are three ways to end a marriage: death, divorce or annulment. If the marriage was not performed according to the formalities required by law, it may be voidable. This means a court can declare the marriage invalid. You should first determine whether you have a valid marriage. All state laws require certain formalities to be followed in order for there to be a valid marriage. First, check to make sure the formalities to marry have been followed in the place where you were married. If the formalities were not followed, the marriage may not be valid.

If you were married in another state or country, the state in which you now reside will recognize the marriage from the other state or country if you complied with the formalities required where you were married. If you were not married in accordance with the formalities of the state or country where you were married, your marriage is not valid and you may not need a divorce unless the state in which you now live recognizes common law marriages (or living together), as a basis for setting forth the legal responsibilities of the parties. Before you jump to conclusions about the validity of your marriage, consult a lawyer and get his professional opinion. The lawyer also will know the proper legal procedure for legally voiding the marriage, if it is necessary in your case.

A ceremonial marriage is required in 37 states in order for a marriage to be legally binding. In Washington D.C. and 13 other states, a marriage can be considered legally binding even when there is no ceremony, if the parties have cohabitated or lived together as husband and wife. This is known as common law marriage. The states which acknowledge common law marriages are Alabama, Colorado, Washington, D.C., Georgia, Idaho, Iowa, Kansas, Montana, Ohio, Oklahoma, Pennsylvania, Rhode Island, South Carolina and Texas. In all other states, both a ceremonial marriage and a marriage license or certificate are required.

In other words, in the states which do not recognize common law marriage, there are no legal rights and duties created by living together. But, if you move, as a couple, from a state that recognizes common law marriage to a state that does not, usually the new state will honor the marriage since the first state recognizes common law marriage. For example, Colorado recognizes common law marriages but Arizona does not. If the common law couple moves from Colorado to Arizona, Arizona law will recognize them to be husband and wife. A word of caution: this area of law is full of pitfalls given the recent changes in the law concerning palimony, prenuptial agreements and non-ceremonial marriage contracts. Some states will recognize and enforce contract rights even though the state laws may not recognize common law marriage. If you have questions, contact an experienced domestic relations lawyer.

In states which do not recognize common law marriage, there are no legal rights and duties created by living together.

Regardless of what rights and duties exist between the parents, the children, whether or not born out of wedlock, are always the responsibility of both parents, unless a court has ordered otherwise. If a parent has abandoned his child, he is still legally responsible for the child's support and can be forced to pay support.

A dissolution of marriage starts by filing a petition or complaint with the court, stating the relevant facts of your case. Before you file your divorce, there are many important decisions to make. Know your options and legal rights before you file your divorce!

No Fault Divorce

There is an alternative to costly lawyers and adversarial proceedings: no fault divorce with an agreed property settlement concerning debts, property distribution, child custody and support. No fault is a simple way to end a marriage without going to war with your spouse, provided you and your spouse are able to work out the details of the divorce. All states and Washington, D.C. have some form of no fault divorce. All you have to allege in the court papers is that the marriage is irretrievably broken or irreconcilable differences have arisen. No fault means that to get a divorce, you do not need to prove that your spouse did something wrong. No fault divorce was implemented to lessen the painful process of nasty divorce proceedings where the parties had to prove certain faults by their spouse. No further proof is required and the parties are entitled to get an order from the court dissolving the marriage.

If one spouse denies that the marriage is irretrievably broken, he may request a mandatory mediation or conciliation conference with the other spouse. Both spouses are then required to appear to determine if they can reconcile their differences. Getting the divorce is easy. How-

A dissolution of marriage starts by filing a petition or complaint with the court.

ever, figuring out what happens to the assets and liabilities of the marriage, who gets custody of the children, and the amount of child support payments or spousal maintenance payments, is difficult. Just because a divorce is a no fault divorce, it does not necessarily mean that it is completely uncontested. An uncontested divorce means that neither spouse takes action to dispute the divorce; you may still have a dispute with your spouse over the property and the debts. This does not affect your right to a divorce. In order to take advantage of no fault divorce, you and your spouse need to agree that the marriage should end. If you can agree on a property settlement, custody, support payments, great! You and your spouse can probably handle your case yourselves. If you can't agree, a judge will decide the matters of property settlement, custody and support. **When you and your spouse can't agree, get legal representation!**

Just because a divorce is a no fault divorce, it does not necessarily mean that it is completely uncontested.

Annulment

Annulment differs from divorce because it is based on problems which existed at the time of the marriage ceremony which make the marriage invalid. Divorce deals with problems which develop between the parties after the marriage. It is similar to divorce because a court order is required to terminate the parties' legal obligations. An annulment results when the judge decides that the marriage was never really a marriage based on the facts discussed below. Divorce is a little different from annulment because the judge decides that there was a valid marriage, however the parties are now entitled to end their marital relationship because of the circumstances. Although the legal effect of annulment and divorce is virtually the same, an annulment is treated as if the marriage never really existed.

Annulment is not as popular as it was in the past because now a divorce is easier to obtain than an annulment. In the past, divorce was very difficult to obtain and the social stigma attached to it was much greater than that of annulment.

Usually, a marriage may be annulled when (1) the parties did not have the legal capacity to marry (for example, two minor children who did not obtain proper consent prior to marrying); (2) one of the parties was previously married and did not have the marriage dissolved prior to remarrying; (3) fraud can be proven; or (4) one of the parties was coerced or forced into the marriage.

The process of annulment is similar to that of divorce.

The process of an annulment is similar to that of divorce. Both are lawsuits filed in court. A summons and petition together with other documents required by the court are filed and served on the other spouse. If it is a contested matter, a hearing will be held wherein the judge listens to both sides and makes a decision on the matter.

In modern annulments, the allegations tend to focus on fraud. Although courts still grant annulments, they may be more difficult to get because the court will require you to prove that the other person lied to you, or misled you about his true circumstances. The concept behind annulment is that the person filing for the annulment never would have consented to enter into marriage had he known the true and important facts about the person he married. If the court agrees, the marriage is legally erased and each party is returned to his former status as a single person.

Remember that the idea behind annulment is that some misrepresentation was made by one party to the other before the marriage, and if the truth had been known there would have been no agreement by the other party to marry. This is important because one spouse can object to an annulment, declaring there was no deception, or that the other spouse accepted the misrepresentation after the marriage.

The idea behind annulment is that some misrepresentation was made before the marriage.

For example, the spouse opposing the annulment may argue that while he is not the religion he told his prospective spouse he was, once married the other spouse accepted the fact without complaint, knowing the truth for months or years after the marriage.

Similarly, if it can be proven that the spouse seeking the annulment actually knew the other spouse's true religion, even though the other spouse lied about it, there will be no annulment. These two defenses against granting an annulment are known as ratification (going along with a problem, without complaint, for a substantial period of time) and actual knowledge (knowing the truth about the spouse, even though the spouse lied).

What is the status of children born from the marriage before there is an annulment? Are the children legitimate? Many states have eliminated legitimacy as a legal concept, and in these states, legitimacy does not matter. In these states, a child born out of wedlock is the natural or legitimate offspring of the parents, according to that state's law. If this is of concern to you, please check with a local attorney concerning your state's law.

CHAPTER TWO
DIVIDING MARITAL PROPERTY AND DEBTS
. . . .

Let's suppose you and your spouse agree that your marriage should end. Now, you must work out the settlement, custody and support issues so the judge can sign the formal order divorcing you, divide the marital assets and award custody and support all at once.

First, the court can dissolve your marriage only if the residency requirements have been met. To file for a dissolution of marriage, one or both of the parties must reside in the state (and sometimes the county) in which they are seeking a dissolution of their marriage. The residency requirements vary from state to state and are anywhere from minimal requirements to residing in the state for one year.

> *The court can dissolve your marriage only if the residency requirements have been met.*

Acting as Your Own Lawyer

You have a right to act as your own lawyer in court. *Pro se* divorces are becoming increasingly more common. *Pro se* or *in properia persona* means on behalf of one's self. It means you are representing yourself without a lawyer. When you have reached agreement with your spouse on the issues of property settlement, custody, child support, and/or spousal maintenance, you are ready to present it to the court for legal approval.

Statistics vary by state, but only about 8 percent to 15 percent of all divorces go to trial. Most of the time, the parties negotiate an agreement and present it to the court for formal approval. In some states, the court has the power to modify the agreement and in other states, the court can only accept or reject the agreement as it is presented by the parties. If the agreement is rejected, the parties are free to renegotiate a new agreement or litigate, that is, to have a trial on the issues over which there is no agreement.

The issues which must be addressed when you get a divorce include: (1) property settlement, including the division of property and debts; (2) child custody and visitation; and (3) child support and/or spousal maintenance. If the request for divorce is contested by the other spouse, or if you can't agree on the property and custody issues, then handling your own divorce is foolish! Hire a lawyer to represent you. However, when you both agree that a divorce is right for you and you want to work out something which is fair, then not using a lawyer may make sense. We still recommend that you get advice about the legal and tax implications of your agreed upon property settlement. This is true even if you intend to present your mutually agreed upon settlement to the court without having a lawyer represent you.

> *If the request for divorce is contested by the other spouse, then handling your own divorce is foolish!*

When determining property settlement, support and custody, keep in mind that the judge will approve what is fair for you, your spouse and the children. The children are the responsibility of both parents so it is important to remember that when children are involved, neither one of the parents becomes divorced from the children, but continues to have parental responsibilities and rights. Try to stay on good terms with the other parent as you will have contact with each other for many years to come. Always consider what is best for the children.

It is always in your best interest to come to some sort of agreement with your spouse to avoid letting the judge decide on the issues. After all, the judge is a stranger to you, your spouse and your children. He will do his best, but there is no guarantee that the order will be fair or satisfactory to you. The judge does not know you, your spouse, your family history or the particular or unique needs of the individuals involved and affected by the divorce. Your goal is to get the judge to adopt your agreement and not create one of his own.

It is in your best interest to come to an agreement with your spouse to avoid letting the judge decide.

In order for the judge to accept your settlement agreement, remember that it has to be fair to everyone concerned, paying particular attention to the needs of the children. Remember this important fact when you are negotiating with your spouse. In order to negotiate a property settlement that the court finds fair, you first need to know what the law in your state says about the rights of property owners.

Community Property

Eight states are subject to community property law; they are Louisiana, Texas, New Mexico, Arizona, California, Nevada, Idaho and Washington. In community property states, each spouse has an undivided one-half interest in all property acquired during the marriage. There is a presumption that all property which is acquired during marriage is community property, and it belongs to the couple. This presumption can be overcome if each spouse treats the other spouse's property as sole and separate, meaning one person's assets are held in his name only.

Each spouse has an equal right to the income and assets of everything earned on behalf of the marital community, even if only one person actually had an income or one person purchased the assets. Similarly, each spouse is equally liable for all the community debts. For example, if you live in Wisconsin, even though it is not a community property state, as of 1986, Wisconsin considers a marital couple's assets and income to be held jointly.

Each spouse has an equal right to the income and assets of everything earned.

Property Rights in States Without Community Property Law

In non-community property states, couples hold property according to that state's laws regarding property. A judge in a non-community property state will divide the property based on what is fair according to the laws of property. In order for a judge to make a fair property settlement, he will look at the rights and obligations of the parties, and how the assets are held. In all states, an asset may be owned in one of three ways:

1. Tenants in Common. This means that each person has ownership rights and the right to control his share. In some cases, spouses may hold unequal shares in the property. When a spouse dies, his share passes to his heirs pursuant to the will of the deceased or according to state law if there is no will. The property will not automatically pass to the surviving owner upon the death of one party.

2. Tenants by the Entirety. This means the spouses together own the property equally. Unlike community property, both spouses must agree to sell it. Creditors of the husband, for example, cannot garnish or put liens against a wife's property, or vise versa if the property is held in tenants by the entirety. Upon death, the property passes to the surviving spouse, not to the deceased spouse's heirs.

3. Joint Tenants. Also referred to as joint tenants with rights of survivorship, wherein each person has an undivided one-half interest in the entire property, and if the other joint tenant dies, the survivor acquires the entire property, and the deceased owner's heirs have no right to that property. Creditors of a joint tenant can obtain interest in the joint tenant's property, or can attach the property if either owner does not pay his bills.

In non-community property states, separate property held by one spouse either acquired before or after marriage can remain that spouse's separate property. In a non-community property state, an inheritance kept in a separate account in that person's name only will remain the property of the person receiving the property.

In non-community property states, separate property held by one spouse can remain separate property.

By contrast, in a community property state, an inheritance becomes community property when it is deposited in a joint account. This is called commingling. Remember, there is a strong presumption that anything either spouse acquires during the marriage is community property if your state follows the community property laws. In community property states, if you want to keep money or other property separate, you must take significant steps to prevent it from being commingled.

Accounts should be designated with your name only as sole and separate property. Do not put your spouse's name on the account or the asset if you intend for it to be your separate property. Do not use these funds to pay for community expenses or to buy community assets. If real property is sole and separate property, and you want it to remain that way, do not include your spouse's name on the deed, because the law will presume that you intended to make a gift of the property to the marital community.

Marital Debts and Property

In a community property state, you have an obligation to pay half of the debts of the marital community as well as a right to receive half of the assets owned by the marital community. Who pays what bills depends primarily on the laws of your state and what the judge thinks is fair under the circumstances. For example, in a community property state, giving husband and wife each one-half of the assets and each one-half of the debts which were incurred to purchase these assets is fair, but it might not be considered fair in a non-community property state when one spouse did not sign for the debt.

Who pays what bills depends primarily on the laws of your state and what the judge thinks is fair.

While there are exceptions, in non-community property states, generally you cannot be held liable for your spouse's debt unless your name is also on the loan document. For example, if a loan is taken out and one spouse has not signed the loan document, the creditor could lose his right to sue the non-signing spouse. However, if the loan was issued to pay for expenses of the non-signing spouse, the judge could order the non-signing spouse to pay the debt.

All debts incurred by the parties during the marriage must be considered in divorce proceedings. Remember, in general, property settlement agreements between divorcing spouses do not curtail the rights of the creditors to whom the accounts are owed. For example, if a couple has a credit card through a local bank while married and in accordance with the property settlement agreement, each agrees to pay half of the balance of the account, but if one spouse fails to make payments, the bank can force the other spouse to pay the balance of the account. The spouse who makes the payments would have a right to collect from the other spouse, but a lawsuit may be necessary to obtain the money.

All debts incurred by the parties during the marriage must be considered in divorce proceedings.

Similarly, if a spouse files bankruptcy after he has agreed to make the payments outlined in the property settlement agreement, the creditor may come to the non-bankrupt spouse for payment of the debt, even though the bankrupt spouse agreed in the property settlement agreement to pay it.

In a community property state, property acquired and money earned by either or both of the spouses during their marriage belongs to both parties usually on a half and half basis, even if the property is in only one of the spouse's names. Separate property is property that either spouse had before the marriage or received as a gift or an inheritance, and it belongs to that spouse only, provided it is not commingled.

If you moved to a community property state after being married in and residing in another state, any property obtained during that period which meets the qualification for community property will be considered community property and split half and half.

Remember, when you and your spouse sign the property settlement agreement, all ownership documents should be executed and recorded in a timely fashion to avoid disputes. Where real estate is concerned, the assignments, notes, mortgages or deeds of trust should be executed and recorded in the County Recorder's Office in the county where the property is located. If automobiles and/or mobile homes are involved, the certificates of title should be properly executed and applications for new titles submitted to the Motor Vehicle Division of the Department of Transportation. If stocks, bonds, and/or other securities are involved, they should be transferred by proper documentation. See your stock broker to retitle securities. It is a good idea to close charge accounts at the time you separate from your spouse to prevent your spouse from running up large amounts of debt.

The division of community property in a divorce must be equitable.

The division of community property in a divorce must be equitable. For instance, while ownership in two automobiles during the marriage might be considered equal, after the divorce, instead of each party keeping half interest in two automobiles, the wife may get one car valued at $6,000 and the husband may get the other car valued at $3,000 together with $3,000 worth of other property. Each party will receive an equitable quantity of the community property. Equitable generally means half.

If you or your spouse have a pension plan, profit sharing plan or retirement account, it may be necessary to obtain a Qualified Domestic Relations Order (QDRO), if you desire to divide the plan between the two of you. To accomplish this, you must either contact a lawyer or the trustee in charge of the plan. Simply listing it on the property settlement agreement will not properly divide the plan. Additionally, you may need professional help from a person such as an actuary to determine the value of a pension so that you can divide it equitably.

You may need help from an "actuary" to determine the value of a pension so that you can divide it equitably.

Guidelines Courts Follow to Determine Property Settlements

The following factors are generally considered by a judge in determining what is a fair and equitable property settlement, although not necessarily in the order listed. In fact, some judges may consider some of these factors almost totally worthless, while other judges may consider a few more important than others. Since state laws are different, some of these factors may not be appropriate. You and your spouse should consider these factors when figuring out what is fair.

The factors may include:

- Future needs of the parties

- The health and age of the parties

- The increased needs of the spouse to whom custody of the children is given

- The amount of income, savings and investments available to each spouse

- Future prospects for earnings for each spouse including income, savings and investments available to each spouse

- Occupational background of each spouse

- The standard of living or lifestyle enjoyed during the marriage

- Relative contributions each made to the marital assets

- Relative detriment each has caused to the marital asset base

- Length of the marriage

Preparing Your Property Settlement Agreement

The first step to preparing a property settlement agreement is to figure out what you own. If you live in a community property state and you have no sole and separate property, everything you own, as well as everything your spouse owns (except his sole and separate property), is considered half yours. The second step is to consider what you owe. Again, if you are in a community property state you are obligated for one-half of all the community debts.

The first step to preparing a property settlement agreement is to figure out what you own.

In a non-community property state, how the property title is held greatly influences what a judge believes to be fair. There is no presumption that all property and liabilities acquired during the marriage are community property and debts, or belong equally to the parties. The judges have latitude in determining how the marital assets and obligations are to be divided.

Special Circumstances to Consider

Waste of Assets

Since you and the court will be focusing on what is equitable, it is important to consider whether some allowance should be made for waste caused by one spouse. In other words, if one spouse has squandered assets of the marriage, for example, by gambling, drinking or poor investments, determine if this waste should be deducted from the squandering spouse's share of the assets, or if the wasteful spouse should be made to pay for the loss. Some states have laws that address this issue. The following states allow the judge to consider one spouse's waste of the couple's assets during marriage in determining the property settlement, custody and support payments: Arizona, California, Colorado, Connecticut, Delaware, Florida, Georgia, Kansas, Illinois, Indiana, Maine, Montana, North Carolina, North Dakota, Pennsylvania, South Dakota, Vermont and Washington, D.C.

Services Provided by a Non-Working Spouse

Consideration also should be made for the value of a non-working spouse's contribution to the household. Some states allow consideration for the efforts of a homemaker, for example, who has prepared meals, tended to the domestic chores and raised the children, to be factored into the settlement agreement. Most states have laws that allow such consideration; however the following states have laws which prevent the judge from considering the value of service supplied by a non-working spouse in determining the property settlement, custody and support payments: Alabama, Hawaii, Idaho, Louisiana, Michigan, New Hampshire, New Jersey, New Mexico, Oklahoma, South Carolina, Texas, Utah and Wyoming.

Consideration should be made for the value of a non-working spouse's contribution to the household.

Wrongdoing By One Spouse Against the Other

Some states allow the property settlement to reflect the emotional pain or suffering one spouse inflicted on the other. In other words, laws in some states give the judge the right to consider the effect of the actions of one spouse, such as an extra-marital affair, a history of physical abuse or mental cruelty, in determining a fair property settlement. States where the judge can consider bad things that a spouse did during the marriage in determining property settlement, custody and support payments include: Alabama, Connecticut, Florida, Georgia, Hawaii, Idaho, Indiana, Kansas, Louisiana, Maryland, Mississippi, Michigan, Nevada, New Hampshire, New York, North Dakota, Pennsylvania (alimony only), South Carolina, Tennessee (alimony only), Texas, Vermont, Virginia (alimony only), Washington, D.C., West Virginia and Wyoming.

Some states allow the property settlement to reflect the emotional pain one spouse inflicted on the other.

Alimony and Spousal Maintenance

Spousal maintenance, formerly called alimony, is sometimes awarded in order to allow a spouse adequate time to become self-supporting, often through furthered education or training. Spousal maintenance is generally considered as temporary support while the spouse gets back on his feet. Your property settlement agreement should state how much money will be paid to the receiving spouse and when the support will cease. The support will usually commence upon the entry of the decree and it will cease on a date you and your spouse agree on, or upon the death, remarriage or sometimes the cohabitation of the receiving spouse. Additionally, the agreement should state that the paying party is entitled to deduct the payment on his income tax returns. The party who receives spousal maintenance must disclose it as income on his tax returns.

Spousal maintenance typically is ordered by the court in order to maintain a standard of living similar to which was accustomed during the marriage. The award of spousal maintenance is no longer given to just the wife. Now, both spouses are eligible to receive spousal maintenance. The law will not look at the sex of the spouse but at one spouse's need for maintenance and the other spouse's ability to pay.

Both spouses are eligible to receive spousal maintenance.

The court will consider maintenance on an individual case basis. Factors include:

- The duration of the marriage

- The age of each spouse

- The skills and education of each spouse

- The parties' standard of living

- Present earning capabilities of the parties

The laws of some states allow the judge to consider marital fault in awarding spousal maintenance. These states are Connecticut, Florida, Kentucky, Michigan, Missouri, Nevada, New Hampshire, North Dakota, Pennsylvania, Rhode Island, South Dakota, Tennessee, Wyoming and Washington, D.C. In some states, the law says that marital misconduct prevents any alimony award. These states are Alabama, Georgia, Idaho, Louisiana, North Carolina, South Carolina, Virginia and West Virginia.

Pension and Profit Sharing

If your spouse has a pension or profit sharing plan, you may be entitled to some of it. Remember that the court will be dividing all of the marital property according to your state's law and the federal law, when applicable. The laws will influence how property or assets held in a retirement account are to be distributed. In other words, you may have a claim to a portion of your spouse's retirement benefits. The first step is finding out if such a plan for retirement exists, the name of the plan, who the administrator is, and the amount of money in the plan. Contact the employer directly for this information or obtain it from your spouse and verify it yourself. If you are not successful, you can get a court ordered subpoena forcing your spouse's employer to provide you with this information.

Similarly, with pension benefits, you must find out if the pension is vested. This means that you must determine if the right to receive the pension exists or will merely exist in the future. Once pension rights are vested, you may have claims under state law to a portion of it, even though your name does not appear on the plan. This is a very technical area of the law which is governed by a federal law called the Employee Retirement Income Security Act (ERISA). Under the law, a spouse is entitled to half of the other spouse's pension where it can be shown that the couple was married for one year before the pension was funded; and the spouse who survives the pensioner has the right to receive the benefits under the terms of the pension plan.

If your spouse has a pension or profit sharing plan, you may be entitled to some of it.

For more information on pensions contact:

Pension and Welfare Benefits
Administration
United States Department of Labor
200 Constitution Avenue N.W.
Washington, D.C. 20210; (202) 523-8233

Pension Rights Center
918 16th Street N.W., Suite704
Washington, D.C. 20006; (202) 296-3776

Social Security

It is possible for a divorced spouse to obtain social security benefits based upon the former spouse's social security earnings record. In order to qualify, the former spouse must be at least 60 years old and the marriage must have lasted for ten years or more. In addition, the law requires that at the time of the application for the benefits, the spouse must be unmarried.

Tax Considerations

Remember that taxes are an important part of any divorce, and should be provided for in a property settlement agreement. If you do a no fault divorce and you are working out your own property settlement agreement, you and/or your spouse may have a tax liability which must be paid. You must not assume that your spouse will pay the liability.

Taxes should be provided for in a property settlement agreement.

You must consider the following issues:

- Whether you will file joint or separate returns

- Who will receive the tax exemption for the

39

children

- Who will be liable for any taxes due

- How will the tax refund be divided

- Who will receive the refund

We recommend that after your property settlement has been worked out, that you contact an attorney or tax accountant to make sure you understand all the tax implications created by your settlement.

Remember, the Internal Revenue Service (IRS) indexes returns based upon both husband and wife's name. If the returns are filed jointly, each spouse is responsible for the entire tax debt for the marital community. A plan to pay any tax liabilities should be worked out with your spouse at the time of the property settlement. That is, decide how much income is yours and how much is your spouse's, and divide it accordingly. This may be modified according to other stipulations you and your spouse reach about payment of certain bills and receipt of certain assets of the marital community.

If the returns are filed jointly, each spouse is responsible for the entire tax debt.

You also may wish to contact a certified public accountant to obtain tax advice about how your divorce will affect your tax situation for the next year. Since you are going from a double income to a single income, and since you will be filing a single return instead of a joint one, there are significant tax consequences which require tax planning. The time to do this is not the following year on April 15th when the taxes are due, but immediately when the divorce settlement is being worked out. What kind of tax planning you do also may influence your property settlement agreement.

Please keep in mind that the IRS considers you married or divorced based on what your status is as of December 31st. For example, if you are married in January of one year and divorced in November of that same year, even though you were married for eleven months, the IRS will consider you to be divorced for purposes of that year, and you must file a single return.

The IRS considers you married or divorced based on what your status is as of December 31st.

Sometimes you will not have the option or the luxury of knowing when your property settlement agreement will be accepted and entered of record. You will not know when your divorce is final because that depends primarily on the judge's calendar and when the divorce decree is signed. Contact your tax accountant and discuss this situation with him so that he can advise you accordingly.

For more information on tax issues concerning divorce call the IRS, whose listing will appear in the telephone directory under U. S. Government, or write for *Community Property and the Federal Income Tax* (publication 555); *Tax Information For Divorced or Separated Individuals* (publication 504); and *Tax Rules for Children and Dependents* (publication 929) available at your local IRS office.

Life Insurance and Medical Insurance

Many divorce agreements contain a provision that the parent obligated to pay support shall maintain a life insurance policy on his life and list the children as beneficiaries. This will provide support to the minor children if their primary supporting parent dies.

Another important insurance issue to consider is medical and dental insurance on the children. You should include a provision in your property settlement agreement stating who will be responsible for insurance and its payment. Another consideration which should be addressed is who will be obligated to pay for any medical or dental expenses which are not covered by the insurance, such as the deductibles.

CHAPTER THREE
DIVORCE SETTLEMENT
ALTERNATIVES

Alternative Dispute Resolution

If you and your spouse cannot come to an agreement with regard to the terms of your divorce, don't give up. You may want to try working out your differences either through conciliation or mediation.

Conciliation

Divorce is not always the answer for domestic problems. Sometimes a marriage can be salvaged with the help of conciliation services. Conciliation is a form of marriage counseling for couples with distressed marital relations. Its primary purpose is to preserve the marriage and to resolve the differences or controversial issues which may have arisen. A professional marriage counselor will coach you and your spouse in working out your problems. Not all couples reconcile after a conciliation conference. If reconciliation does take place, it is the decision of both parties. The counselor is there to help you, but will not force you to reconcile if it is not your desire to do so.

> *The primary purpose of conciliation is to preserve the marriage by resolving controversial issues.*

Mediation

Mediation is another way to resolve disputes without a court room battle, with regard to such issues as custody, property settlement, support and division of debts. An agreement in mediation can be reached only when the parties have determined in advance that their marriage relationship is ending and that they will disregard all questions of marital fault. Mediation is a voluntary process which uses the help of a neutral third party who is a trained counselor to help the parties reach an agreement. The third party can be a professional mediator, a family counselor or member of the clergy. The mediator is not a judge and will not make decisions for the parties or advise the parties what they should do on any issues.

There are some guidelines involved in mediation. For example, the parties must agree to full disclosure and no relevant information will be withheld. The subject of mediation is limited to resolving issues on property division, support and parenting arrangements, or any other matters arising out of the impending divorce.

Mediation is limited to resolving issues on property division, support and parenting arrangements.

During the mediation process, the parties discuss their desires and plans as well as the future needs of their children, focusing on the future and not the past. The mediator is trained in conflict resolution and guides you through the process of working out your own agreement as to child custody, property division, visitation and spousal maintenance. Mediation usually takes an average of six to ten hours.

Mediation is not marriage counseling, is not a substitute for obtaining legal advice, and is not used to get you back together with your spouse. You should look at mediation as a positive step taken to resolve your disagreements which will direct you and your spouse to a fair divorce settlement. Mediation can be a very favorable step to resolving your differences quickly, cost effectively, and without having to resort to an adversarial proceeding. You will find that after attending mediation, the stress and anxiety often associated with divorce can be reduced significantly.

Legal Separation

If you and your spouse agree to separate but you are not sure if you want a divorce, a legal separation may be an alternative. In order for a legal separation to be binding, a petition for legal separation must be filed with the court and a court order signed by a judge. Legal separation is similar to divorce because you address division of property and debts, child support and custody, and spousal maintenance during the separation period.

You may wonder why someone would want to go through the trouble of obtaining a legal separation if it's basically the same as a divorce. There are a few reasons. First, some couples may not desire to divorce because of religious reasons. Second, if one spouse has legal or financial troubles, you may not want to be held liable for your spouse's actions. Third, you may not be ready for divorce but feel you need to legally separate from your spouse while deciding if you really want a divorce.

If you legally separate from your spouse and you later decide to get a divorce, the divorce proceedings are much easier. Often, all that is required after the entry of an order of legal separation is submitting a divorce decree to the court. We recommend you contact a competent domestic relations lawyer for help in this area.

Separation can create significant legal problems. Leaving your spouse and not continuing to

If you legally separate from your spouse and later decide to get a divorce, the proceedings are much easier.

live together is a ground for a no fault divorce. The key issue is whether the separation was voluntary, and problems in determining what is voluntary sometimes occur in interpreting someone's action. For example, if someone moves out because he felt he had no choice, is the action voluntary? Or, what about the spouse who is away because of military service or hospitalization?

Generally, the courts hold that a separation is voluntary if it is based upon mutual consent at the time of the separation. For example, if a spouse joins the Peace Corps at the start of the separation period, the court is likely to find the separation voluntary. By contrast, if the husband is drafted and moves out to report to boot camp before there is an agreement that the spouses wish to separate, then the separation is not considered voluntary.

Each state's law is a little different in this area. "Voluntariness" generally depends upon the circumstances you find yourself in, as well as your state's case law. The difficulty is in trying to interpret people's actions, so the courts look at objective factors when determining whether the separation was voluntary. As you can see, there can be problems when the issue becomes one party's word against the other's.

The courts look at objective factors when determining whether the separation was voluntary.

Therefore, it is a good idea to prepare a document, which both of you sign, setting forth the terms of the separation and the date it is to become effective. Also, be sure to state in the document that the separation is a mutual and voluntary desire of both parties.

Please keep in mind that most states which consider living apart as a ground for a no fault divorce do not require that the spouses leave voluntarily. This is because their laws do not require proof of voluntariness. These state's are: Arkansas, Connecticut, District of Columbia, Hawaii, Idaho, Maryland, Nevada, New Hampshire, New Jersey, North Carolina, Oklahoma, Pennsylvania, Rhode Island, South Carolina, Texas, Vermont, Virginia and West Virginia.

Please note that New Hampshire has special rules, so check with your local lawyer if you live there.

Since this is a complicated area, we suggest that you contact a local, licensed attorney and tell him the facts of your case. Even if you do not want to hire a lawyer and cannot afford one, many lawyers will help you understand the law on a particular issue and charge you only for their consulting time. Do not be deterred from getting a lawyer's advice because you feel you can't afford to pay him to handle the entire legal proceeding. You may wish to do as much as possible on your own, and then contact an attorney to review the papers or provide help in a particular area, such as determining what your state law says about voluntariness and no fault. Remember, we recommend hiring a lawyer in every case, except where both parties are in agreement on all issues, and each is prepared to cooperate with the other in good faith and follow through by filing the appropriate legal documents and going to court.

Many lawyers are willing to help you understand the law and charge you only for their consulting time.

CHAPTER FOUR
CHILD CUSTODY, VISITATION AND SUPPORT

In General

In determining the rights and duties of parents, it is important to recognize that all states require both parents to share the responsibility of supporting their children. The parent who has physical custody of the children usually is entitled to monetary support for the children. Every parent must support his child, whether or not the couple was married when the child was born. A parent is not excused from providing child support by thinking that, since the parties are not married, an obligation to support no longer exists.

> *Every parent must support his child, whether or not the couple was married when the child was born.*

How much support must be paid depends on the child support guidelines in your state. To obtain these guidelines, call the clerk of the court in your county, district or parish.

Your state most likely has visitation guidelines which set forth the minimum visitation allowed to the non-custodial parent. If both parents agree, additional visitation can usually be arranged between the parties.

The primary responsibility for the education, care and control of the children remains with the parent granted custody. If the parents have difficulties in communication and are unable to reach an agreement as to who should have custody of the children, the court will decide the custody issues. When courts decide custody, various statutory factors must be considered in order to determine whether an award of custody to the father or mother, or joint custody will best serve the interests of the children. In making a custody determination, courts may not discriminate against either parent because of gender. Basically, the parent awarded custody will have demonstrated he is better able to care for the children. If the parents are unable to come to a decision about custody, it may be wise to have a lawyer or a mediator help—before you go to court.

Tips on Custody

A judge may award custody of your children to you or your spouse, or to both of you jointly with visitation rights to the non-custodial parent, unless there are very extreme circumstances involving child abuse.

As stated in the section on property settlement, remember that it is better to work out your own custody and visitation schedule than to have the judge impose his idea of fairness on you and your children. Whenever you are dealing with custody issues keep in mind that the best interests of the children are paramount.

When dealing with custody issues, keep in mind that the best interests of the children are paramount.

In a perfect world, this section would not be necessary; in fact, this book would not be necessary. Because divorce is a reality and children often are involved, here are some helpful tips you should know about when dealing with custody issues:

- Never, ever, under any conditions, bad mouth your spouse in front of the children. Talk to your lawyer, your counselor or your friends about your spouse, but not to the children. No matter what wrong your ex-spouse has committed, there is simply no benefit you will ever receive by expressing your ill feelings about your ex-spouse to the children.

- Be polite, but careful in dealing with your ex-spouse. Anything you say, write or do could be used against you as evidence of your unsuitability to be a custodial parent. The best way to handle this is to assume that every conversation you have with your ex-spouse could be taped, and a copy of everything you write or send to your ex-spouse could be seen by a judge. Assume that a judge is watching over your shoulder every time you have contact with your spouse!

- Focus on defining your strengths rather than your spouse's weaknesses. The judge is not uninformed, so credit him with the ability to understand the situation at hand without complaining about everything your spouse has done wrong.

- Never use custody or visitation as a means of gaining leverage for what you want from your spouse, such as the house, property, money, etc. The courts will not look favorably on this type of behavior.

- When you visit or have custody of the children always be a good parent. Don't do things to intentionally irritate your spouse such as not bathing the children or clothing them inappropriately. Don't tell your

Never use custody as a means of gaining leverage for what you want from your spouse.

children things to intentionally upset your spouse.

- If you cannot agree on custody and visitation, try mediation, counseling, arbitration or some other alternative instead of a custody battle in court. Such court contests are not only expensive, costing between $3,000 and $10,000 or more, but they cause hatred, bitterness and frustration whether you are on the winning or losing side, and the children suffer the most.

- Lastly, as with everything else involving the law, **put it in writing.** If you have a visitation schedule worked out, put it in writing. Both of you should sign it and submit it to the court with a request for it to become part of a formal court order.

Joint Custody

Many states have adopted rules allowing joint custody. Some states even allow a judge to award joint custody against the wishes of the parents. Joint legal custody is where the parents share legal custody and neither parent has superior rights to the children. Joint physical custody means the physical residence of the child is shared with both parents and substantial time is spent with each parent.

Joint custody is where the parents share legal custody and neither parent has superior rights to the children.

Joint custody is a parenting plan which usually provides significantly more decision making, custodial time and control between the parents than is provided in sole custody arrangements. When parents are awarded joint custody they share equally in the authority and responsibility for making decisions with regard to the upbringing of the minor children. Generally, the child spends a substantial amount of time, but not necessarily equal time, with each parent. One parent's home is often designated as the principal residence of the child.

Parents desiring to obtain joint custody should have a history of cooperation and similar values concerning the children, and both parents must have been caretakers for the children. Keep in mind that joint custody means you will have a continuing relationship with the other parent, even after the divorce is final.

Parents desiring to obtain joint custody should have a history of co-operation.

— If you desire to have joint custody, the agreement should specifically state at least the following: (1) with whom the child will reside and when; (2) visitation for each parent; (3) any restrictions on either parent moving out of the city, county or state with the child; (4) education and religious training; (5) a means to resolve financial responsibility for specific expenses and (6) a means to resolve disputes concerning the children.

Depending upon the particular circumstances of your case, there may or may not be a basis for deviation from the child support guidelines as a result of joint custody.

You may be required to meet with your spouse at the conciliation court prior to your court hearing if you desire joint custody. Call the domestic relations division in the court clerk's office for more information on joint custody. Please note however, that joint custody is subject to approval by the court and each individual case is reviewed separately by the court. In most states, law permit judges to consider the preferences of the child. However, Arkansas, Maryland, Massachusetts, Mississippi, New York, North Carolina, Oregon, Pennsylvania, Rhode Island, South Carolina and Vermont do not allow judges to consider the preference of the children.

Sole Custody

In the past, the courts often viewed the mother as the better parent to care for the minor children. Years ago, for a father to get custody of the children often meant that he had to prove the mother unfit to care for the children.

Now, the law in most states does not presume either parent to be better able to care for the children. Both parents are presumed to be equally qualified to be awarded custody. If the parties cannot agree on custody, the court will decide who is the better custodial parent for the children.

Both parents are presumed to be equally qualified to be awarded custody.

Visitation

The parent who does not receive custody of the children almost always is given reasonable visitation rights unless the court decides that visitation will seriously endanger the child's physical, mental or emotional health. Reasonable visitation rights mean visitation at times and places which fit into the personal schedule of the child and which do not unreasonably interfere with the schedule of the custodial parent.

The following information may be helpful in determining a reasonable visitation schedule.

- It is typical for the non-custodial parent to be granted overnight weekend visitation and extended summer visitation. The length of such periods depends on the ages and personal schedules of the children.

- The key to a successful visitation schedule is regularity, consistency and flexibility.

- Both parents should extend courtesy to one another in planning and carrying out visitation. The visiting parent should inform the other of where the children are and if there were any problems with them. Each party should notify the other of any variations in plans.

Also, your state may have guidelines which will help you formulate a visitation plan that is appropriate for your circumstances.

Keep in mind that criminal and civil penalties can be brought against a person who keeps or hides a child in order to frustrate custody or visitation orders. If a parent believes that he is being refused reasonable visitation, that parent may petition the court for assistance or consult a lawyer.

In addition to providing financial support, parents also have the obligation not to abuse their children.

Visitation and child support are two separate issues. Denial of visitation is not allowed because of non-payment of child support.

Parental Rights and Duties

In addition to providing financial support for children, parents also have the obligation not to abuse their children. Most states have severe criminal penalties for child abuse. Generally child abuse is broadly defined by statute to include a parent's failure to provide adequate shelter, food, clothing, medical treatment, discipline, etc. In order to determine what constitutes child abuse in your state, you should review your state's statutes. These are easy to find at any public library. Ask the librarian for help. You should review the criminal code, the juvenile code, and any statutes which relate to children.

The law requires doctors, teachers, workers, and policemen to report child abuse. Most states' laws carry immunity for such reports, meaning that even if the report is wrong or exaggerated, the parents cannot sue the person making the report, even if the claim turns out to be totally unfounded. The idea is to encourage the free reporting of potential child abuse so that it can at least be investigated. The government has an interest in protecting the child if the parents will not. The reason for this is that the government is acting as an overseer for the children, who in theory may have been neglected by the parent.

The law requires doctors, teachers, and policement to report child abuse.

For more information on child abuse, contact:

> The National Center on Child Abuse and Neglect
> Department of Health and Human Services
> P.O. Box 1182; Washington, D.C. 20013
> or call (202) 245-0586

If you are concerned about a missing child, a number of agencies may be of help, including:

> Missing Children Help Center
> 410 Ware Blvd., Suite 400
> Tampa, Florida 33619
> or call (813) 623-KIDS or 1-800-USA-KIDS

National Center for Missing and Exploited Children
2101 Wilson Blvd., Suite 550
Arlington, Virginia 22201
or call 1-800-843-5678

National Runaway Switchboard
3080 North Lincoln; Chicago, IL 60657
1-800-621-4000

Child Support Laws: Determining a Fair Amount for Support

The law states that both natural parents are obligated to support their minor children until the age of majority which is 18 or 21, depending upon the laws of your state. The parents must provide food, clothing, medical care, shelter and education for their children. These same laws apply for parents of adopted children as well. Under the Family Support Act of 1988, a federal law, all states have increased their child support enforcement efforts.

Collection of child support is one of the biggest problems parents face after a divorce.

Collection of child support is one of the biggest problems many parents face after a divorce. Laws have been enacted over the past several years in an effort to correct this problem. In most cases, the non-custodial parent, meaning the parent who does not have physical custody, will be ordered to pay child support to the custodial parent.

Child support is determined by the supporting parent's income or in some instances, what he is capable of earning. If the parent obligated to pay support is not working, then his obligation may be based upon a full time job at minimum wage. Most states have written criteria and guidelines for support. An example of an income schedule adopted in Arizona as a guideline for fixing child support is included in this chapter. Remember **these are merely guidelines** and the court bases its support award on circumstances of each case and each child's unique needs. Each state is required to have its own guidelines, which may or may not be similar to Arizona's.

If the income level of either parent changes in the future, a court order is requested to change the amount of support paid. In addition to determining the child support obligation based upon the income of the parties, and their ability to pay, the court also will look at the needs of the child. Additional support may be allocated if the child is handicapped, requires special education, is specially gifted, or if excessive expenditures are necessary. Other factors include medical care and day care expenses.

Another important child support factor to remember is that even if you and your spouse agree to a certain sum of support, the court always has the final authority. This means that the court may order additional child support even if not requested. It is likely that the court will not approve your settlement agreement if you don't provide for adequate child support.

Even if you and your spouse agree to a certain sum of support, the court has the final authority.

To obtain more information about child support, write to:

The Office of Child Support Enforcement
Department of Health and Human Services
370 L'Enfant Promenade SW
Washington, D.C. 20447
or call (202) 401-9370

ARIZONA CHILD SUPPORT GUIDELINES

Monthly Combined Adj. Gross Income	Number of Children					
	One	Two	Three	Four	Five	Six
$ 700	$ 55	$ 56	$ 56	$ 57	$ 57	$ 58
800	121	123	124	125	127	128
900	162	190	192	194	196	198
1,000	178	256	259	262	265	268
1,100	193	299	327	330	334	338
1,200	209	324	395	399	403	407
1,300	224	347	435	465	470	475
1,400	240	372	465	525	538	544
1,500	256	396	496	559	607	613
1,600	271	420	526	593	647	683
1,700	287	444	558	627	685	731
1,800	300	465	582	656	716	764
1,900	313	485	607	684	747	797
2,000	326	505	632	712	778	830
2,100	338	525	657	741	808	863
2,200	350	543	680	767	837	894
2,300	361	560	700	790	862	921
2,400	372	576	721	818	887	948
2,500	382	592	741	836	913	976
2,600	392	608	761	858	936	1,000
2,700	403	624	781	881	961	1,026
2,800	413	640	801	904	986	1,053

ARIZONA CHILD SUPPORT GUIDELINES

Monthly Combined Adj. Gross Income	Number of Children					
	One	Two	Three	Four	Five	Six
$ 2,900	$ 425	$ 656	$ 821	$ 926	$ 1,011	$ 1,080
3,000	434	672	842	949	1,035	1,106
3,100	445	684	863	974	1,082	1,134
3,200	456	707	886	999	1,089	1,164
3,300	468	725	908	1,024	1,116	1,193
3,400	479	742	930	1,048	1,143	1,222
3,500	491	760	952	1,073	1,170	1,251
3,600	502	778	974	1,098	1,197	1,280
3,700	513	795	998	1,123	1,224	1,309
3,800	525	813	1,018	1,148	1,252	1,338
3,900	536	830	1,040	1,173	1,279	1,367
4,000	548	848	1,062	1,198	1,306	1,396
4,100	559	866	1,085	1,223	1,333	1,425
4,200	570	883	1,107	1,248	1,360	1,454
4,300	582	901	1,129	1,273	1,387	1,483
4,400	593	918	1,151	1,298	1,414	1,512
4,500	605	937	1,174	1,324	1,443	1,543
4,600	618	956	1,198	1,351	1,472	1,575
4,700	628	973	1,219	1,375	1,498	1,602
4,800	640	991	1,242	1,401	1,526	1,632
4,900	652	1,009	1,266	1,426	1,554	1,662
5,000	663	1,026	1,286	1,449	1,579	1,689

Enforcing Child Support Payments

According to figures released by the United States Census Bureau in October, 1991, about half of the American men ordered to pay child support in 1989 and 1990 failed to pay as ordered, and approximately one-fourth of the men ordered to pay support paid nothing at all. Sometimes fathers don't pay the amount they have been ordered to pay by the court because the amount they have been ordered to pay is unrealistically high. Some fathers have experienced severe economic hardship and simply do not have the resources to pay the child support ordered. If the father's financial situation changes, he can and should go to the court where the support was ordered and request that a modification of the child support be made, based on his current income and expenses.

Keep in mind that collecting support payments depends upon the ability to pay.

For those fathers who have the money but refuse to pay, a court hearing is necessary to request the judge to order back support payments or to authorize the seizing of his assets in order to convert them to cash to pay the support. Keep in mind that collecting support payments depends upon the ability to pay. If he does not have the ability to pay, all the court orders in the world won't matter. If you do not know whether he has any money or assets, you may want to hire an investigator to do an asset check. An asset check is done by a private investigator who examines court and other public documents, motor vehicle records, etc. in order to determine whether there are any assets available out of which the support payments could be paid. Costs to conduct an asset check depend on what needs to be done, and may be as low as $75, or as high as $400.

Secondly, you must keep in mind that if you are going to bring an action for support, you must have legal papers served on the person whom you want to pay. This means that you must know where he lives or where he can be located in order to have him served. If you do not know this information, you may have to hire an investigator to perform a skip trace. Again, fees vary widely, but this can cost as little as $75 or as much as several thousand dollars, depending on the complexity of the search. We do not recommend that you try to obtain either a skip trace or an asset check on your own without a lawyer. It is better to hire the lawyer who knows investigators who are effective and cost efficient.

If a parent fails to pay child support, it is possible to obtain a court order to garnish his wages. In most states there is a procedure for child support garnishment via wage assignment in which the court orders an employer to pay wages directly to the court, which in turn pays it to parent or guardian of the minor. It is also possible to attach or garnish bank accounts belonging to the non-paying parent or attach other property that he owns. The property is then sold, and the proceeds are turned over to the court, which in turn, gives the money to the parent or guardian of the child.

If a parent fails to pay child support, it is possible to obtain a court order to garnish his wages.

Skip tracing, asset checking, and collecting child support by garnishment or attachment are all expensive and complicated. If you cannot afford a lawyer, call your local Legal Aid Society listed in the telephone directory to determine if you are eligible for a Legal Aid lawyer. If Legal

Aid won't take your case, call your local county or district attorney, or the attorney general of your jurisdiction (listed under State Government in the telephone directory) and ask to speak with someone in the Child Support Enforcement Division.

You also may wish to contact your local social services commission for help. It also is listed under State Government in the telephone directory, or call:

Office of Child Support Enforcement
Department of Health & Human Services
425 I St., N.W., Room 3
Washington, DC 20001; (202) 724-8800

What To Do if You Are Not Receiving Child Support

Many courts have developed simplified child support enforcement procedures which are designed to be used without the assistance of a lawyer. Court clerks should be able to provide assistance in obtaining and filing the appropriate forms. Often the forms are pre-printed and are available through the clerk of the court.

Courts have developed simplified procedures designed to be used without the assistance of a lawyer.

Most states have adopted the *Uniform Enforcement of Child Support Act*, which makes applying for an order of the court enforcing payments easier. This federal law can be found at 42 USC 651. You can review this law at your local library, just ask the librarian for the U.S. Code.

Check with the court clerk in your state to determine if your state follows the uniform act and whether the court issues a wage assignment or a withholding order which requires an employer to withhold support payments out of the employee's paycheck. If a wage assignment is used, the employer will then mail it to the court clerk who will then forward it to the recipient spouse. Even if your ex-spouse isn't working, a wage assignment can be used to attach income from many other sources such as unemployment checks, pensions, retirement accounts and other benefits.

Another way to get back child support paid to you is to intercept your ex-spouse's federal income tax refund. This is very helpful if your spouse lives in another state and other collection efforts have failed. But **do not forge his name!** Contact a lawyer about what to do after getting the return. Other things to consider in collecting support include obtaining a judgement for back support and filing a lien on his property. If the lien is properly filed and the property is sold, the lien must be paid from the proceeds of the sale. Because your state's law may be complicated in these areas, it is advisable to get a lawyer to help you.

Another way to get back child support paid is to intercept your ex-spouse's federal income tax refund.

You also can have your spouse held in contempt of court for failure to pay support pursuant to a court order. This requires going back to the judge, who ordered child support in the first place, and filing papers. If all else fails, consider criminal prosecution. Many states make it a crime not to pay child support, which could be punishable by imprisonment.

There are several government agencies which can help you collect support. Contact the Child Support Enforcement Administration, or a similar agency. Check your telephone directory for a local county listing. They will provide assistance with enforcement and collection of support.

Child Kidnapping

Every year more and more children are victims of child snatching by parents who are not entitled to legal custody. Often, the motive behind the child snatching is animosity felt by one parent toward the other. Before you take your child from the custodial parent, consider that the abduction is likely to have a long term effect on your child. In addition, the Parental Kidnapping Act is designed to discourage parental abductions, and it provides for severe penalties against parents who kidnap a child. If you fear that your child might be kidnapped by your ex-spouse, talk to a lawyer to be advised of your legal rights.

If your child has been kidnapped, try to stay calm but call the police immediately!

If your child has been kidnapped, try to stay calm but call the police immediately! You should contact your ex-spouse's employer, his friends, neighbors, in-laws, or anyone who knows your spouse and might have information as to the whereabouts of your spouse and children. Do not take the law into your own hands, but instead consider filing charges against your spouse. You also may be entitled to recover damages against your ex-spouse for expenses you have incurred and compensation for emotional distress.

What happens when a parent takes a child to another state without permission or in violation of a court order? Which state's law applies? These kinds of issues fall under the heading of jurisdiction. Because questions about which state's law applies are thorny, and because state laws relating to custody may be different from each other and often conflict, you need a lawyer to help you if your child has been taken to another state.

However, a uniform law has been adopted in a majority of states which is designed to eliminate these jurisdictional problems, and crack down on parents who steal their children and run to another state. It is called the Uniform Child Custody and Jurisdiction Act. This is a very important law, but trying to comply with its provisions, such as providing notice, can be confusing and complicated for someone who has no lawyer, If you are involved in a situation where the act applies, a domestic relations lawyer should be able to help. Look in the Yellow Pages under Attorneys; under subcategories of Divorce and Domestic Relations.

Paternity

If a father refuses to acknowledge parenthood, in order for the court to order child support, it must first be proven that he is the child's natural father. In order to obtain a court order of support, the court must hear evidence which establishes a link between the child and the father. In establishing fatherhood, the mother will have to bring a suit in court. These suits are called paternity suits. There is only one issue, and that is the identity of the child's father.

Paternity cases may involve blood tests. However, blood typing does not establish that John Doe is Baby Doe's father. All it does is reveal whether a man could not have been that particular child's father. The problem with blood typing is that it cannot prove that the man is that

The problem with blood typing is it cannot prove the man is a particular child's father, only that he could be.

particular child's father, only that he could be; therefore, it is only a screening test.

The new approach is to use Human Leucocyte Antigen (HLA) testing which, in essence, compares blood types, tissue types, and genetic profiles in order to establish an identity between the father and the child. The courts also have accepted the use of DNA typing. In essence, this test compares the basic building blocks of cell tissue of the father with that of the child in order to determine whether a particular person is in fact that child's parent.

Assuming a court finds that a man is the child's parent, and orders support, the father no longer can claim that he has no obligation. If the court rules in favor of the mother's claim, even though the man continues to deny parenthood, the court's order will require him to pay child support in an amount established in your state, and assume parental responsibilities for the child.

The court has the power to jail a non-complying parent upon a finding of contempt of court if the parent refuses to pay child support. This also applies to parents who were once married. Check with a lawyer in your state to learn more about the laws which may apply in your case.

The obligation to provide child support ends when the child reaches the age of majority. In some states support continues until the end of the school year for children who turn 18 during their senior year in high school. The age of majority is either 18 or 21, when the child is considered to be an adult and is no longer considered a minor by law.

Termination of Parental Rights

Every state has laws which can strip a parent of his rights and obligations with respect to his own children. Who can bring these cases usually depends on whether the person bringing the suit has some blood relationship to and/or substantial interest in the child's welfare. Every state has laws which permit the state itself to file such a request with the court.

In every case of termination, there must be a court hearing, and the person or the state seeking to end the parental relationship must show, at the hearing, that the parent is either unfit or has abandoned his child, and that it is in the best interest of the child to have the parental rights terminated. The grounds for termination vary among the states, as does what kinds of facts tend to establish fitness. But all states require that the offending parent be given an opportunity to explain his side of things and to cross-examine all of the witnesses who are called against him.

Please keep in mind that judges do not terminate parental rights easily. What is unfit requires strict proof. It is not enough simply to show that the child might be better off without the parent. In addition to unfitness or abandonment, it also must be shown that it is in the child's best interest not to have the parent involved in the child's life any longer. In this area, you must get a lawyer!

Every state has laws which can strip a parent of his rights and obligations with respect to his own children.

Caution!

First, a word of caution. We recommend proceeding without a lawyer **only** in an uncontested no fault divorce and **only** if all of these conditions exist:

1. You and your spouse have the patience and the fortitude to deal with each other and to negotiate your own settlement, custody and support arrangements, and you are both able to put it in a form that is necessary for the court. You also must be able to follow through by going to court when necessary.

2. You lack the money to hire a lawyer, or you don't feel a lawyer is necessary in your case.

3. Neither of you has retained a lawyer.

With respect to point number 3 above, be careful! **If one spouse has a retained lawyer, do not represent yourself—hire a lawyer immediately.**

Documents such as assignments or releases should be prepared or reviewed by a lawyer.

We also recommend you contact a lawyer or tax accountant to make sure you understand all the tax and legal implications of your settlement and custody agreement. Any other documents, such as assignments or releases, should be prepared or reviewed by a lawyer.

Remember we are talking about acting as your own lawyer only in a very limited circumstance: uncontested, no fault divorce. No fault divorce involves one party defaulting or not formally answering court papers after the parties have agreed on all of the important issues. **If your spouse has a lawyer and has served papers on you, you must not allow a default to be taken against you until you have talked to your own lawyer, not your spouse's lawyer.**

Ignoring court papers prepared by your spouse's lawyer or signing papers prepared by your spouse's lawyer because you think your spouse or his lawyer would not mislead you, could have detrimental results.

First, work out the details of the divorce, such as property settlement with your spouse; next, see a lawyer to make sure you did everything right; then, file your papers.

Preparing Your Own Divorce— Getting Started

The following is a step by step outline and explanation of how a typical no fault divorce is processed without a lawyer. These procedures are general and are not precisely the same in every state. Remember to obtain the valid forms from the court, a lawyer, a reputable forms supplier or document preparation service before filing your divorce. We feel this section is invaluable in explaining the system, defining terms, and describing the mechanics step by step, but remember every state is different! This outline may not be accurate for your state, but it is a helpful illustration. So make sure you find out your state's procedures before you file!

Obtain the valid forms from a reputable source before filing your divorce.

Even if you and your spouse unanimously agree to the divorce and terms, it still is a good idea to at least see a lawyer for legal advice before you prepare your divorce papers. There may be some laws that affect you of which you are not aware. A set of sample necessary divorce forms is contained in this book, however these forms may differ from state to state. These forms are copyrighted and are provided only as an example and are not to be copied or retyped. Check with the court clerk in your county to find out where you can purchase the required forms and make sure those forms will be accepted by the court. Many bookstores, stationery stores and document preparation services sell do-it-yourself kits which contain all the forms necessary to complete a no fault divorce. Make sure you use only the forms which are for your state.

It's a good idea to consult a lawyer for legal advice before you prepare your divorce papers.

Typical No Fault, Default Forms Used in Court

No fault, default divorce means that both parties agree to the terms of the divorce and sign the necessary papers. The respondent (the person who the divorce is filed against) generally does not have to make a court appearance or file a response, thereby defaulting. The petitioner (the person initiating the divorce) appears in court, testifies, and submits a Decree of Dissolution of Marriage and Property Settlement Agreement to the court, which is signed by both parties. When the court signs the Decree of Dissolution and the clerk of the court enters it in its records, the divorce is final and the marriage is dissolved.

A no fault divorce means that neither party alleges fault on the other party, but simply states that the marriage is irretrievably broken or that irreconcilable differences have arisen. To help you obtain a no fault, default divorce, a list of the typical documents needed to complete the divorce and an explanation of the forms are set forth below. Because the laws and procedures do vary from state to state, you should check with a lawyer or the court clerk in your county. **DO NOT USE THE FORMS REPRODUCED IN THIS BOOK**; they are included only as an illustration to help you understand the process of no fault divorce, so that you can ask the proper questions of your attorney before you file in your state.

1. Domestic Relations Cover Sheet: This form, which is usually obtained from the Clerk of the Court, states the petitioner's and respondent's names, addresses and if there are minor children involved, their names and dates of birth. If spousal or child abuse is involved in your case, it is usually not necessary to reveal your whereabouts or address on documents filed with the court.

If spousal or child abuse is involved in your case, it is usually not necessary to reveal your address.

2. Summons: This form is issued by the court (although you must prepare it) and is notice to the respondent that he has a certain period of time, usually 20 days if he lives in state or 30 days if he lives out of state, in which to respond to the lawsuit. If he does not respond, then default may be entered against him. The court clerk will issue the summons and return the original to you.

3. Petition For Dissolution of Marriage: This document asks the court to dissolve the marriage and also states the pertinent facts relative to the case. In addition, it sets forth the petitioner's requests with regard to custody, spousal maintenance, and an equitable division of property and debts.

4. Preliminary Injunction: This document gives notice to the parties that they cannot transfer or conceal any property; they cannot harass each other; and they cannot remove the minor children from the state. This injunction is generally effective upon the petitioner as soon as the case is filed with the clerk of the court, and it is effective as to the respondent as soon as he is served or signs an acceptance of service.

5. Notice of Right to Convert Health Insurance: This document gives notice to the parties that they have the right to keep their health insurance after the divorce by converting the policy to their own policy and by agreeing to pay the premiums. Also, health insurance must be maintained after the filing of the petition through the date of the divorce.

In most states, you must make a court appearance and testify before your divorce will be granted.

6. Notice of Information to Conciliation Court: This document gives notice to the court of the petitioner's and respondent's names and addresses and the names of any minor children born of the marriage. Again, if abuse is involved, you may not wish to divulge your address and/or telephone number.

7. Application for Entry of Default: This document states that the respondent has not filed a response to your petition to dissolve the marriage within the time allowed by law, and it requests the court to enter default against the respondent. After this document has been filed, and a copy mailed to the respondent, then the petitioner may call the court to schedule a hearing date for the divorce.

8. Decree of Dissolution of Marriage and Property Settlement Agreement: At the time of the hearing, the petitioner must take the Decree of Dissolution of Marriage and Property Settlement Agreement to court. The court will review the documents at the hearing and if the court agrees, the judge or commissioner will sign the decree and the parties will be divorced when the signed decree is entered of record by the clerk of the court. However, entry of the decree by the clerk may not occur on the same day that the judge signs the decree.

9. Parental Worksheets: The worksheets state the income of the parties and what the child support obligation will be. All child support is paid through a wage assignment whereby the support obligation will be deducted from the non-custodial parent's wages and paid through the court to the custodial parent. At the divorce hearing, the judge will sign the order for child support and the obligation will begin at that time.

Once you have your papers completed and you are ready to file the papers with the court, the procedure is simple. You may first want to check with the court clerk and see if there are instructions available from the clerk on how to process or handle your own divorce. If not, check your packet of forms, as there should be detailed instructions of what to file, where and when to file it.

Once you have your papers completed and ready to file, the procedure is simple.

The first set of documents to file include the summons, petition for divorce, the injunction, notice of information to the conciliation court, and health insurance notice. The petition tells the court you are filing for divorce and what you want the court to order with regard to support, custody and property settlement. After you file these papers and the court confirms (or stamps) them, then you will need to give a copy of these papers to your spouse and obtain his signature on the acceptance of service, property settlement agreement, and divorce decree. If your spouse won't accept service (by signing the acceptance of service) you will have to have him served by a licensed process server. Also, if he won't accept service, this may be a sign that you need to consult with a lawyer. Usually a certain waiting period is necessary before you can go to court to obtain the final divorce decree.

Important note: If your spouse files a written response with the court, you cannot proceed with the divorce filings by default. See a lawyer right away!

What to Expect in Court

In most states, you must make a court appearance and testify before your divorce will be granted. Some states have modernized the proceedings and eliminated the requirement to appear in court in simple uncontested, no fault cases which meet certain requirements.

You will be required to testify under oath regarding the allegations contained in your petition for divorce.

You will be required to testify under oath regarding the facts and allegations contained in your petition for divorce. The judge may ask you questions relative to the proceedings. Be concise with your answer, but answer the questions fully. Additionally, the judge probably is not interested in your specific domestic troubles, so don't offer this information unless you are asked. Just answer the questions truthfully and briefly.

Plan to be at the hearing early to give yourself time to locate the courtroom and to have the necessary documents ready for the judge. Some courts have the clerk of the court review your papers before you enter the courtroom so that everything is in order for the judge.

It is a good idea to sit in and observe a divorce hearing prior to your court date. This will help you understand what will happen at your hearing and inform you as to the documents you will need and what questions will be asked. You will feel more comfortable knowing ahead of time what will take place at your hearing.

Lastly, and most importantly, is courtroom etiquette. You must show respect and patience for the court. You should always behave in a courteous manner. Appropriate dress in a courtroom is required. No shorts, halter tops, or tank tops should be worn. When speaking to the judge, you should address him as Your Honor.

Once the judge signs your divorce decree and the clerk enters it in his records, you are legally divorced.

Once the judge signs your divorce decree and the clerk enters it in his records, you are legally divorced. Be sure to follow the final checklist in Chapter 6 to tie up any loose ends regarding your divorce.

```
_____
_____
_____
[Phone] _____
```

SUPERIOR COURT OF ARIZONA, County of Maricopa

In re the Marriage of:)
) No. _____
_____,   )
          Petitioner,   )   S U M M O N S
and   ) (Domestic Relations)
)
_____,   )
          Respondent.   )
_____   )

              THE STATE OF ARIZONA TO: _____

          YOU ARE HEREBY SUMMONED and required to appear and
defend, within the time applicable in this action in this Court.
If served within Arizona, you shall appear and defend within 20
days after the service of the Summons and Petition upon you,
exclusive of the day of service. If served out of the State of
Arizona, whether by direct service, registered or certified mail,
or by publication, you shall appear and defend within 30 days
after the service of the Summons and Petition upon you is
complete, exclusive of the day of service. Service by registered
or certified mail outside the State of Arizona is complete 30
days after the date of filing the receipt and affidavit of
service with the Court. Service by publication is complete 30
days after the date of first publication. Direct service is
complete when made. RCP, A.R.S. Sections 25-311 to 25-381.22.
          YOU ARE HEREBY NOTIFIED that in case of your failure to
appear and defend within the time applicable, judgment by default
may be rendered against you for the relief demanded in the
Petition.
          YOU ARE CAUTIONED that in order to appear and defend,
you must file a proper response in writing with the Clerk of this
Court, accompanied by the necessary filing fee, within the time
required. You are required to serve a copy of any response upon
the Petitioner. RCP 10(d), A.R.S. Section 12-311, RCP 5.

          The name and address of the Petitioner is:

                         _____
                         _____
                         _____

                         SIGNED AND SEALED this date_____
                         _____
                         Clerk
                         By_____
                            Deputy Clerk

76

```
_____
_____
_____
```
In Pro Per

SUPERIOR COURT OF ARIZONA

COUNTY OF MARICOPA

In re the marriage of:)
)   No. _____
_____,   )
)
            Petitioner,   )   PETITION FOR DISSOLUTION
)   OF MARRIAGE
and   )
)   (With Minor Children)
_____,   )
)
            Respondent.   )
_____)

      Petitioner, appearing pro per, alleges as follows:

      1. Petitioner and/or Respondent have been (i) domiciled (or stationed, while a member of the armed services) in the State of Arizona, and (ii) residing in the County in which this Petition is filed, for more than ninety (90) days immediately preceding the filing of this Petition.

      2. Petitioner's Name: _____
         Petitioner's date of birth: _____
         Petitioner's occupation: _____
         Petitioner's current address:
         _____

         Petitioner's length of domicile
           in Arizona: __ yrs.

      3. Respondent's name: _____
         Respondent's date of birth: __-__-__
         Respondent's occupation: _____
         Respondent's current address:
         _____

         Respondent's length of domicile

1

in Arizona: __ yrs.

4. Date of Marriage: __-__-__

5. Place of Marriage: _____, __

6. Wife is not now pregnant.

7. The marriage is irretrievably broken, there being reasonable prospect for reconciliation.

8. The conciliation provisions of Title 25 of t Arizona Revised Statutes either do not apply or have been met

9. Neither Petitioner nor Respondent is in the milita service of the United States of America.

10. This Court has jurisdiction over this matter.

11. Petitioner and Respondent are each able to provi for their own support, and neither requests spousal maintenanc

12. Regarding children:

(a) The minor child(ren) common to this marriage, the birth dates, the person(s) primarily responsible for their ca and custody during the last five years (if no entry appears, sa care and custody was jointly with Petitioner and Respondent), a their addresses of residence for the last five years are follows:

Child	Birth Date	Custodian	Residence	Period of Time

(b) Petitioner has not participated as a party witness, or in any other capacity, in any other litigati

2

78

concerning the custody of the minor child(ren) in this or any other state.

(c) Petitioner has no information of any custody proceeding concerning the child(ren) pending in a court of this or any other state.

(d) Petitioner knows of no other person, not a party to these proceedings, who has physical custody of the child(ren) or claims to have physical custody or visitation rights with respect to the child(ren).

(e) The custody of the child(ren) should be awarded as set forth in the prayer herein which is believed to be the best interests of the child(ren), all with reasonable visitation to the party not having custody.

13. The custodial parent is in need of an award of child support, as well as orders for medical insurance for the child(ren) and payment of any non-covered reasonable medical, dental or health related expenses.

14. The parties have accumulated certain community and common property, and debts during the course of their marriage, and no agreement has yet been made as to the disposition of these assets and liabilities.

15. Wife desires to have her former name restored to her pursuant to A.R.S. §25-325(c).

WHEREFORE, Petitioner requests that this Court:

1. Decree a dissolution of the parties' marriage.

2. Approve the Property Settlement Agreement and any

3

other formal written agreements the parties have entered into, and in the event the parties have not reached a formal written agreement, enter such order as to the disposition of property, debts, and attorneys' fees and costs as the Court deems just and equitable.

3. Award custody of the minor child(ren) as follows, with reasonable visitation rights to the non-custodial parent:

Child	Custodial Parent
_____	_____
_____	_____

4. Order the non-custodial parent to pay to the custodial parent a reasonable amount for the support of the minor child(ren).

5. Assign the responsibility for providing medical insurance coverage for the minor child(ren) and for paying any medical expenses of the child(ren) not covered by said insurance.

6. Restore Wife's former name of _____.

7. Grant such other and further relief as the Court deems just and proper under the circumstances.

STATE OF ARIZONA   )
) ss.
County of Maricopa   )

I have read the foregoing Petition For Dissolution of Marriage and know of my own knowledge that the facts stated therein are true and correct, except as to those matters alleged

. . .

. . .

4

80

on information and belief, and as to those matters, I believe
them to be true.

_____
[Signature of Petitioner]

SUBSCRIBED AND SWORN to before me by the Petitioner on
this date _____.

_____
Notary Public

My Commission Expires:

_____

SAMPLE

5

81

```
_____
_____
_____
_____
```

In Pro Per

SUPERIOR COURT OF ARIZONA

COUNTY OF MARICOPA

In re the Marriage of:)
)   No. _____
_____,   )
                  Petitioner,   )   PRELIMINARY INJUNCTION
)   AGAINST BOTH PETITIONER
)   AND RESPONDENT
and   )
)
)
_____,   )
)
                  Respondent.   )
_____)

IMPORTANT - YOU SHOULD READ THIS COURT ORDER IMMEDIATELY!

Pursuant to order of the Presiding Judge of the Superior Court of the State of Arizona, in and for the County of Maricopa in accordance with A.R.S. 25-315(A), as amended 1977, Ch. 138, Section 6 and amended 1980, Ch. 113, Section 2:

IT IS ORDERED that during the pendency of this action, YOU, PETITIONER AND RESPONDENT, named above as parties to this action, are enjoined from and shall not:

1.   Transfer, encumber, conceal, sell or otherwise dispose of any of the joint, common, or community property of the parties except in the usual course of business or for necessities of life, without the written consent of both parties or permission of the Court;

2.   Molest, harass, disturb the peace of, or commit an assault or battery on the person of your spouse (Petitioner or Respondent) or any natural or adopted child of the parties; or

3.   Remove from the State of Arizona any natural or adopted child of the parties presently residing in the State of Arizona without the prior written consent of both parties or permission of the Court.

IT IS FURTHER ORDERED that this Injunction is effective against both parties to this action. If you are the Petitioner, the Injunction is effective upon filing the Petition for Dissolution or Legal Separation. If you are the Respondent, this

Injunction is effective upon being served with, or accepting services of a copy of this Injunction upon you.

IT IS FURTHER ORDERED that this Injunction has the same force and effect as an order of the Superior Court signed by a Judge and enforceable by all remedies made available by law, including contempt of Court.

WARNING - OFFICIAL COURT ORDER!

If you disobey this Order the Court may find you in contempt of Court. You may also be arrested and prosecuted for the crime of interfering with judicial proceedings and any other crime you may have committed in disobeying this order.

You or your spouse may file a certified copy of this Order with your local law enforcement agency. A certified copy may be obtained from the Clerk of the Court that issued this Order. If you are the person that brought this action, you must also file evidence with the law enforcement agency that this Order was served upon your spouse.

This Court Order is effective until a final Decree of Dissolution or Legal Separation is filed or the action is dismissed.

ISSUED UNDER MY HAND AND SEAL of this Court on the _____ day of _____, 19__.

Clerk of the Superior Court

By: _____
    DEPUTY CLERK

2

83

```
_____
_____
_____
_____

In Pro Per
```

SUPERIOR COURT OF ARIZONA

COUNTY OF MARICOPA

```
In re the Marriage of        )
                             )   No. _____
_____,          )
                             )   NOTICE OF RIGHT TO
            Petitioner,      )   CONVERT HEALTH INSURANCE
                             )
    and                      )
                             )
                             )
_____,          )
                             )
            Respondent.      )
_____)
```

This notice is given pursuant to A.R.S. Sections 20-1377 and 20-1408 and is provided to the petitioner in order that the parties to marriage dissolution are aware of a dependent spouse's right to continuance of health insurance coverage under existing group or individual policies. This notice shall be served on the respondent together with the petition, summons, and preliminary injunction.

Coverage provided by a conversion policy must provide benefits most similar to the coverage in the policy, but may contain less coverage at the option of the dependent.

Children may also be covered at the option of the dependent spouse who has responsibility for care and support of the children.

Conversion is not available to a person who is eligible for Medicare or other similar disability benefits which together with the conversion would constitute overinsurance. However, dependent children of a person eligible for Medicare may be covered by a conversion or continuation.

The dependent spouse must notify the insurance company of the conversion or continuation of coverage and pay the monthly premium within thirty-one (31) days of the date coverage would otherwise terminate.

84

_____
_____
_____

In Pro Per

SUPERIOR COURT OF ARIZONA

COUNTY OF MARICOPA

In re the Marriage of:)
)   No. _____
_____,   )
           Petitioner   )   PETITIONER'S DECLARATION
)   OF INFORMATION FOR
and   )   CONCILIATION COURT
)
_____,   )
           Respondent.   )
_____)

       Pursuant to Local Rules of Maricopa County Superior Court, Petitioner herewith submits the following information to the Clerk of the Superior Court for delivery to the Director of the Conciliation Court:

NAME OF PETITIONER: _____

MAILING OR BUSINESS ADDRESS: _____
_____

NAME OF RESPONDENT: _____

MAILING OR BUSINESS ADDRESS: _____
_____

THE RESPONDENT IS BEING SERVED BY: _____

MINOR CHILDREN BEING AFFECTED BY THIS CAUSE ARE:
_____

       DATED this _____ day of _____, 19___.

_____
[Signature of Petitioner]

```
_____
_____
_____
```

In Pro Per

SUPERIOR COURT OF ARIZONA

COUNTY OF MARICOPA

In re the Marriage of:)
)   No. _____
_____,   )
)
                    Petitioner,   )   APPLICATION FOR ENTRY OF
)   DEFAULT, AFFIDAVIT ON DEFAULT
and   )   AND ENTRY OF DEFAULT
)
_____,   )
)
                    Respondent.   )
_____)

STATE OF ARIZONA   )
) ss.
County of Maricopa)

        The undersigned, being first duly sworn, deposes and

says:

        1. The affiant is the Petitioner in the above entitled

cause of action; that no answer or other pleading has been served

upon affiant by the Respondent _____, or filed

with the Clerk of the Court;

        2. That the statutory time as provided by law,

exclusive of the date of service, has elapsed since the service

of a copy of the Summons and Complaint herein on the above named

Respondent;

        3. That the Respondent is not in the military service

        4. That a copy of this application for entry of default

was mailed by first class mail, postage prepaid, to the person

named below at the address indicated:

86

```
_____
_____
_____
_____
In Pro Per
```

                        SUPERIOR COURT OF ARIZONA

                           COUNTY OF MARICOPA

In re the Marriage of:)
)   No. _____
_____,   )
)
            Petitioner,   )   ACCEPTANCE OF SERVICE
)   OF PROCESS
and   )
)
_____,   )
)
            Respondent.   )
_____)

        The   undersigned,   _____,   hereby
acknowledges receipt of and accepts service of a true copy of the
Summons, Petition for Dissolution of Marriage, Preliminary
Injunction, Notice of Right to Convert Health Insurance and
Notice to Conciliation Court, issued in this action, such
acceptance to have the same effect as if a true copy of the above
documents had been served upon the Respondent by a duly
authorized process server as of the date of this acceptance.

        DATED this _____ day of _____

                              _____
                              [Signature of Petitioner]

STATE OF ARIZONA   )
) ss.
COUNTY OF MARICOPA   )

        The foregoing instrument was acknowledged before me this
_____ day of _____, 19__, by _____.

My commission expires:

_____   _____
                              Notary Public

_____
_____

WHEREFORE, affiant prays that default be entered against the above named Respondent.

DATED this _____ day of _____, 19____.

_____
[Signature of Petitioner]

SUBSCRIBED AND SWORN TO before me this ___ day of _____, 19____.

_____
Notary Public

My commission expires:
_____

ENTRY OF DEFAULT

In this action, the above named Respondent having been regularly served with process and having failed to appear and answer the Petitioner's complaint on file herein, and the time allowed for answering having expired, the default of the Respondent, _____ is hereby entered, effective ten (10) days from the filing of the foregoing application, unless the Respondent pleads or otherwise defends herein as provided by the Arizona Rules of Civil Procedure within ten (10) days of the date of the foregoing application.

WITNESS my hand and seal of the Superior Court this ____ day of _____, 19_____.

_____, Clerk

By_____
Deputy Clerk

2

1

2 In Pro Per

3   SUPERIOR COURT OF ARIZONA

4   MARICOPA COUNTY

5 In re the Marriage of:)
6 _____   )   No. _____
)
7   Petitioner,   )   DECREE OF DISSOLUTION
8 and   )   OF MARRIAGE
)
9 _____   )   (With Minor Children)
)
10   Respondent.   )
11 _____)

12   THIS MATTER coming to be heard by this Court without a

13 jury,

14   THIS COURT FINDS:

15   1. Petitioner has filed with this Court a Petition For

16 Dissolution of Marriage, and Petitioner and/or Respondent had

17 been domiciled (or stationed, while a member of the armed

18 services) in the State of Arizona for more than ninety (90) days

19 immediately preceding the filing of said Petition.

20   2. Respondent was duly served with a copy of the

21 Summons and Petition for Dissolution of Marriage, Preliminary

22 Injunction, Notice of Right to Convert Health Insurance and

23 Petitioner's Declaration to Conciliation Court, and has failed to

24 file a response, and default has been filed and validly entered

25 against Respondent.

26   3. The marriage is irretrievably broken, there being no

89

reasonable prospect of reconciliation.

4. The conciliation provisions of Title 25 of the Arizona Revised Statutes either do not apply or have been met.

5. The parties have entered into a Property Settlement Agreement (the "Agreement") concerning the division of their property, payment of their obligations, spousal maintenance, child custody and support, if applicable, and other matters, which Agreement is attached hereto and hereby made a part hereof as if set forth in full herein.

6. The Agreement is not unfair to either party, and it contains provisions appropriate under the circumstances as to spousal maintenance and child support and visitation.

THEREFORE, IT IS ORDERED, ADJUDGED AND DECREED:

1. The marriage of the parties is dissolved and each party is restored to the status of a single person.

2. The Agreement is hereby approved and confirmed, but not merged into this Decree, and relief is granted as is set forth therein. The parties are ordered to comply in all respects with the terms of the Agreement. The Agreement is incorporated into and made a part of this Decree; provided, however, that the Agreement shall not merge into this Decree and shall remain in all respects binding upon the parties and shall be enforceable as a contract, in addition to any enforcement of its terms available as part of this Decree.

3. Custody of the minor child(ren) of the parties shall be and is awarded as follows, with the principal residence of

2

90

said child(ren) being with the custodial parent:

CHILD   CUSTODIAL PARENT

_____   _____

_____   _____

    4. The Court hereby adopts the worksheet which is attached to this Decree as the findings of the gross income, adjusted gross income, basic child support obligations, total child obligations, each parent's proportionate share of the total child support obligations, and the amount of the child support award. The Court orders the non-custodial parent to pay to the custodial parent, on the first day of each month, the sum of $_____ per month as and for child support, commencing with the first day following the issuance of this Decree by this Court, and continuing until one of the minor child(ren) shall have reached the age of majority, or shall die, at which time, and each time thereafter that a child reaches the age of majority or dies, the child support obligation shall be revised in accordance with the Maricopa County Child Support Guidelines then in effect. In case a child reaches the age of majority while attending high school, child support shall continue past the age of majority and be paid to the custodial parent during the period of time in which the child is actually attending high school, but not beyond June 1 of the school year during which such child reaches the age of majority.

    5.   Husband and Wife shall exchange financial

3

91

information, including but not limited to, federal and state income tax returns, spousal affidavits, earning statements and financial statements, every twenty-four (24) months commencing twenty-four (24) months after the date of this Decree. All financial information shall be kept confidential, except as may be needed in domestic relations proceedings. The Court further authorizes that if a written request for such information is not complied with, a subpoena duces tecum shall be issued.

6. All child support payments shall be made through the Clerk of the Maricopa County Superior Court, and shall be increased by and shall include any fees charged by said Clerk in connection with said payments, and shall be paid through a wage assignment. Payments not made through said Clerk shall be considered gifts unless otherwise ordered by the Court. The non-custodial parent shall notify said Clerk of any changes to his/her address or the name and/or address of his/her employers or other payors within ten (10) days of any changes thereof.

7. Health and dental insurance shall be maintained for the benefit of the minor child(ren) as follows:

CHILD   RESPONSIBLE PARENT

_____   _____

_____   _____

Medical and dental expenses not paid by insurance shall be paid by the parties as follows:

4

CHILD	HUSBAND'S %	WIFE'S %
_____	_____%	_____%
_____	_____%	_____%

8. Said payments shall be made through the Clerk of the Maricopa County Superior Court, and shall be increased to include and shall include any fees charged by said Clerk. Payments not made through said Clerk shall be considered gifts unless otherwise ordered by the Court. Husband shall notify said Clerk of any changes to Husband's address or the name and/or address of Husband's employers or other payors within ten (10) days of any changes thereof.

9. The following other relief is granted:_____ None _____

_____.

DONE IN OPEN COURT this date:_____ SAMPLE _____

_____
Judge/Commissioner

APPROVED AS TO FORM AND CONTENT:

_____
[Signature of Petitioner]

_____
[Signature of Respondent]

5

93

_____
_____
_____
_____

In Pro Per

SUPERIOR COURT OF ARIZONA

COUNTY OF MARICOPA

In re the Marriage of:)
)   No._____
_____,   )
)   PROPERTY SETTLEMENT
            Petitioner,   )   AGREEMENT
)
and   )
)   (No Minor Children)
_____,   )
)
            Respondent.   )
_____)

      1.   <u>PROPERTY TO HUSBAND</u>. The following property shall be the property of Husband, as his sole and separate property, and Wife shall execute all documents necessary to deed and assign all her right, title, and interest therein to Husband.

      a.   Cash, bank accounts, certificates of deposit and similar property, as follows:

Institution	Account Number or Other Identification	Approximate Value

      b.   Stocks, bonds, other securities and similar accounts, as follows:

Asset	Identification No.	No. of Shares or Face Value	Approximate Total Value

      c.   The personal effects and household goods, furniture, and furnishings listed on Husband's Personal Property Inventory attached hereto.

      d.   Motor vehicles and boats, as follows:

Make	Model	Identification No.

          e. Real property and related improvements, as follows:

          f. Business interests as follows: (name of business,
type of business, i.e., corporation, partnership, sole
proprietorship, and percentage of interest):

          g. Insurance policies:

     Type   Insurer   Policy Number   Face Amount

          h. Retirement plans as follows (type of plan, name of
plan, trustee of plan, nature of interest):

          i. Other property as follows (describe sufficiently to
identify):

          All personal property presently in the possession of
Husband and not expressly included in Section 3 below.

          2. DEBTS TO BE PAID BY HUSBAND. The following debts
shall be solely the obligations of Husband, who shall pay the
same as they become due:

Creditor   Description of Debt   Approximate Balance

Husband shall further be obligated to pay such other debts as he
has incurred since the parties have been living apart, and all
debts which are liens or encumbrances against any property
awarded to Husband hereunder or otherwise belonging to Husband,
if the same are not listed in Section 4 below.

          3. PROPERTY TO WIFE. The following property shall be
the property of Wife, as her sole and separate property, and
Husband shall execute all documents necessary to deed and assign
all his right, title, and interest therein to Wife.

          a. Cash, bank accounts, certificates of deposit and

                              2

similar property, as follows:

Institution	Account Number or Other Identification	Approximate Value

      b. Stocks, bonds, other securities and similar accounts, as follows:

Asset	Identification No.	No. of Shares or Face Value	Approximate Total Value

      c. The personal effects and household goods, furniture, and furnishings listed on Wife's Personal Property Inventory attached hereto.

      d. Motor vehicles and boats, as follows:

Make	Model	Identification No.

      e. Real property and related improvements, as follows:

      f. Business interests as follows (name of business, type of business, i.e., corporation, partnership, sole proprietorship, and percentage of interest):

      g. Insurance policies:

Type	Insurer	Policy Number	Face Amount

      h. Retirement plans as follows (type of plan, name of plan, trustee of plan, nature of interest):

      i. Other property as follows (describe sufficiently to identify):

      All personal property presently in the possession of Wife

3

96

and not expressly included in Section 2 above.

4. **DEBTS TO BE PAID BY WIFE.** The following debts shall be solely the obligation of Wife, who shall pay the same as they become due:

| | | Approximate |
| Creditor | Description of Debt | Balance |

Wife shall further be obligated to pay such other debts as she has incurred since the parties have been living apart, and all debts which are liens or encumbrances against any property awarded to Wife hereunder or otherwise belonging to Wife, if the same are not listed in Section 2 above.

5. **SPOUSAL MAINTENANCE.** Husband shall pay Wife spousal maintenance as follows:

6. **WIFE'S NAME.**

Wife's name shall be restored to her former name of _____.

7. **MISCELLANEOUS PROVISIONS.**

(a) The parties each represent that all property, real or personal, wherever located and however denominated, has been disclosed to the other party and mentioned and dealt with in the conversations leading up to the execution of this Agreement.

(b) The parties shall henceforth hold, possess, and enjoy for his or her sole and separate use, free from interference and control by the other, all of the real and personal property which he or she owns upon execution of this Agreement, or may hereafter acquire.

(c) Except as expressly provided herein, Husband and Wife agree to assume as his or her sole and separate obligation, any debt incurred by him or her after the date of this Agreement, and to pay and hold the other free and harmless from any liability or cost, including reasonable attorneys' fees, created thereby, or by the defense or resolution of any such debt.

(d) Each of the parties hereby waives, releases, and forever discharges the other party, his or her heirs, executors,

4

97

administrators, assigns, property and estate, now owned or hereafter acquired, from any and all rights, claims, demands, and obligations of every kind and character arising out of or by virtue of the marital relation of the parties, including without limitation, in the event of death, intestate or testate, the right of inheritance, descent, distribution, rights of election against the other's will, and the right to act as legal representative of the estate of the other; provided, however, that nothing herein contained shall constitute a waiver by either party of any rights which that party may acquire in the future by any agreement executed by the parties hereto, or anyone else, including the right to receive a voluntary bequest under the will of the other executed subsequent to the date hereof.

(e) The parties hereto agree to indemnify, defend, and hold each other harmless from any loss, claim, demand, or liability, including without limitation the payment of any attorneys' fees and costs incurred by virtue of the other party failing to perform any provision of this Agreement, breaching any warranty herein, or failing to pay any amounts as agreed to herein. All amounts so owing shall bear interest at a rate of eighteen percent (18%) per annum from the date of accrual, until paid.

(f) Notwithstanding any provisions herein contained to the contrary, the agreements of the parties as contained in this Agreement are and shall continue to be binding contractual obligations, forcible as such, notwithstanding the incorporation of this Agreement into a decree of dissolution of marriage. Such incorporation shall not effect or constitute a merger of the provisions of this Agreement into a decree of dissolution of marriage so as to preclude the enforcement of the contractual obligations herein contained in a separate proceeding maintained for such purpose.

(g) Any modification or waiver of any term of this Agreement, including a modification or waiver of this term, must be in writing and signed by the parties to be bound by the modification or waiver.

(h) In the event any portion of this Agreement shall be declared by any court of competent jurisdiction to be invalid, illegal, or unenforceable, such portion shall be deemed severed from this Agreement, and the remaining parts hereof shall remain in full force and effect as fully as though such invalid, illegal, or unenforceable portion had never been part of this Agreement.

(i) The parties each agree to do such further acts and things and to execute and deliver such additional agreements and instruments as either party may reasonably require to consummate, evidence, or confirm the agreement contained herein in the manner

5

98

contemplated hereby. Notwithstanding the foregoing, it is agreed that this Agreement is intended to be, and shall be construed to be, a sufficient conveyance, assignment, transfer and bill of sale of any and all rights, title, interest, claim and demand of every nature covered by this Agreement.

(j) This Agreement may be filed by the parties in the pending action for the dissolution of the marriage of the parties in the Maricopa County Superior Court for approval thereof by said Court. Each party expressly represents that this Agreement is made and entered into freely and voluntarily by each of the parties, free from any duress, constraint or influence of any kind or nature on the part of the other, and expressly represents that this Agreement is fair. The parties request that the Court approve this Agreement as the settlement agreement of the parties.

(k) Except as may otherwise be expressly set forth herein to the contrary, this Agreement (including any Exhibits attached hereto), along with any other papers filed in the marriage dissolution proceedings of the parties, constitutes the entire agreement between the parties with respect to the subject matter hereof and supercedes all prior understandings, if any, with respect thereto. The parties do not intend to confer any benefit hereunder to any person, firm, or corporation, other than the parties hereto. No representation, warranty, or agreement herein may be relied upon by any person not a party to this Agreement. There are no oral promises, conditions, representations, understandings, interpretations or terms of any kind as conditions or inducements to the execution hereof, or in effect between the parties, except as may otherwise be expressly provided herein.

(l) This Agreement and all representations and warranties contained herein, or in any certificate or other document delivered pursuant to this Agreement, shall survive the making of this Agreement and shall be binding upon the parties thereafter.

(m) This Agreement shall be governed by, interpreted under and construed and enforced in accordance with the laws of the State of Arizona, and has been reached by fair negotiation, and shall not be construed against either party as a result of any drafting efforts of the parties.

(n) If arbitration or other legal action is instituted hereunder, the prevailing party in such action shall be entitled to recover from the other party its reasonable attorney's fees and costs.

(o) This Agreement constitutes a settlement document, shall not constitute an admission of any fact by either party hereto, and shall not be admissable in any proceeding except a proceeding commenced to enforce any rights under this Agreement or

6

99

resulting from any alleged breach of this Agreement.

8.   OTHER PROVISIONS.

(a)   Any debts not allocated to the parties under Section 3 and 4 above, or any other provision of this Agreement, shall be the responsibility of the parties, each as to one-half.

(b)   Each party shall pay the cost of any attorney hired by such party.

THE PARTIES ACKNOWLEDGE AGREEMENT to all of the foregoing provisions of this Property Settlement Agreement, as of the _____ day of _____, 19___.

Petitioner:_____

Respondent:_____

List of Attachments:

Husband's Personal Property Inventory
Wife's Personal Property Inventory

7

100

What If I Need a Lawyer?

Sometimes the best way to find a lawyer is to ask your friends if they have used a lawyer or know a good lawyer who handles domestic relations matters. You can get first hand information on how good the lawyer is by talking to one of his former clients. Remember that you are paying him and it is your decision whether or not to retain a certain lawyer.

You can get first hand information on how good the lawyer is by talking to one of his former clients.

It is important that you discuss the lawyer's fee with him before hiring him, and make sure you understand the fees which will be charged and that you are satisfied. Don't pay or retain him until you are sure. Consider telling the lawyer you will call him in a day or two, if you need time to think about it.

If you cannot find a lawyer, call the County or State Bar Association in your area and ask if they have a lawyer referral service. Many states have such a service and they will make an appointment for you with an attorney who is experienced in the area of your legal problem. There may be a nominal fee for the first consultation, so inquire about any fees before you make an appointment.

Information to Take When You See a Lawyer

On the following pages you will find two handy charts specifying information you will need when you visit the lawyer. Fill in the blanks!

Information to take when you see a lawyer, (chart 1)

ITEM	HUSBAND	WIFE
Full legal name	----------	----------
Date of birth	----------	----------
Social Security Number	----------	----------
Address	----------	----------
Occupation	----------	----------
Employer	----------	----------

	CHILDREN	
	Name	Age
Date of marriage	----------	
Place of marriage	----------	----------
Date parties separated	----------	----------
Reason for divorce, (optional)	----------	----------
Does wife wish to restore maiden name?	----------	----------

Information to take when you see a lawyer, (chart 2)

ASSETS

Home(s) _ _ _ _ _ _ _ _ _ _ _ _ _ _ _ _
Automobile(s) _ _ _ _ _ _ _ _ _ _ _ _ _

_ _ _ _ _ _ _ _ _ _ _ _ _ _ _ _ _ _
Bank account(s) _ _ _ _ _ _ _ _ _ _ _ _
Insurance policy(s) _ _ _ _ _ _ _ _ _ _ _
IRS/Retirement Acct's _ _ _ _ _ _ _ _ _ _
Stocks/bonds _ _ _ _ _ _ _ _ _ _ _ _ _ _
Partnerships/businesses _ _ _ _ _ _ _
Furniture _ _ _ _ _ _ _ _ _ _ _ _ _ _ _

_ _ _ _ _ _ _ _ _ _ _ _ _ _ _ _ _ _
Major Household Items _ _ _ _ _ _ _ _

_ _ _ _ _ _ _ _ _ _ _ _ _ _ _ _ _ _

INCOME

Husband _ _ _ _ _ _ _ _ _ _ _ _ _ _ _ _
Wife _ _ _ _ _ _ _ _ _ _ _ _ _ _ _ _ _ _

DEBTS

	Creditor	Amount	For
1.			
2.			
3.			
4.			

LIVING EXPENSES

	Item	Amount	For
1.			
2.			
3.			
4.			

CHILDREN'S SPECIAL NEEDS

	Item	Amount	For
1.			
2.			

Note: Bring copies of tax returns, brokerage accounts, bank accounts and deeds to real estate.

CHAPTER SIX
AFTER THE DIVORCE
....

How to Establish Credit After Divorce

Sometimes it is difficult to establish credit after a divorce because one of the spouses was better able to show assets or income necessary to obtain credit. The spouse who has relied on the ex-spouse's income or assets for credit may feel left out in the cold. Until the enactment of the federal Equal Credit Opportunity Act (ECOA), it was very difficult for the dependent spouse to obtain credit after a divorce. This was because credit agencies and creditors generally looked at the credit rating of the stronger spouse and assigned that credit rating to the couple. The dependent spouse would then have no history which would be significant enough to justify the extension of credit.

ECOA was intended to resolve this problem. The act prevents discrimination because of race, color, religion, national origin, sex, age, or marital status. This means that the act prevents creditors from disallowing credit simply because a divorced spouse has no credit history apart from that established as a couple. However, the act still requires that the spouse meet the lending guidelines of the creditor. In other words, if you qualify for a loan, you are entitled to receive it under the ECOA, regardless of the fact that you may never have had credit in your own name before this application. The idea is not to punish or affect a person's credit rating simply because

> *The ECOA prevents creditors from disallowing credit simply because a divorced spouse has no credit history.*

of the change in marital status. You also should be aware that it is illegal under the ECOA for a creditor to ask whether you are married on a loan application. It is perfectly normal for the creditor to ask if the loan will be taken in one or two names, but it is not appropriate to ask about marital status in determining whether the loan should be granted.

There are a number of ways to establish credit after you have been divorced. The first step is to obtain a credit card in your own name and pay it off each month. You can obtain a list of banks who will provide credit cards without annual fees from:

Bankcard Holders of America
560 Herndon Parkway, Suite 120
Herndon, VA 22070, (703) 481-1110

The key to successful managing of credit obligations after a divorce is to remember to charge only small items so that you are able to pay them off within thirty days of the purchase. This takes careful planning and management. In other words, instead of paying cash for the purchase of a set of towels, for example, you may elect to put them on your credit card. Then, write a check for the full amount of the purchase and keep it with your bills to be paid. This way you have already deducted the price of the charged item from your account. When you receive your bill in approximately thirty days, simply mail the check to the creditor and the credit reporting agency will show a successful credit transaction. In addition, you will not be bothered by excessive credit balances.

The key is to charge only small items that you are able to pay off within thirty days.

Another option is to obtain a co-signer, such as a parent or a friend, on a loan. As long as the debt service payments are made on a timely basis, when the purchase has been paid off (the debt satisfied), your credit report will reflect this payment history, and you will be given credit for paying off the loan.

Another avenue to establish credit history is to apply for a loan using your savings account as collateral.

Another possible avenue of obtaining a favorable credit rating and good credit history after your separation or divorce is to apply for a loan at your bank using your savings account as collateral. Don't buy anything! Take the loan proceeds, deposit it into your savings, and pay off the loan within two to three months. You will lose the amount that you have to pay for interest, but remember that your loan will be earning interest in savings. Your net loss should be very small, since the loan will be small, and you will pay it off entirely within two to three months. The transaction, however, can help you gain a valuable credit history. Consider it an investment in your future!

CHECKLIST

After Your Divorce is Final

_____ Obtain a certified copy of the Divorce Decree or Order of Dissolution from the court. (You may be able to get this at the time of the divorce hearing.)

_____ Make sure that all documents necessary to transfer ownership or interest in property to the party entitled to ownership and quit claim deeds are recorded with the county recorder where the property is located.

_____ Contact creditors to advise them which party is responsible for paying debts and making arrangements to remove the name of the spouse who is not responsible for those debts.

_____ If you requested that the court restore your former name, then change your name on your credit cards, bank accounts, driver's license and social security card.

_____ Close and split joint accounts as agreed in the Property Settlement Agreement.

_____ Contact the Department of Motor Vehicles to change titles to all vehicles.

_____ Make arrangements to prepare and execute a new Will.

Optional:

_____ Record the decree with the County Recorder if you own real estate.

Index

A

Abduction (see Kidnapping by parent)

Abuse (see Domestic violence)

Accountant, 40

Actuary, 33

Adultery (see Divorce, grounds for)

Age of majority, 66

Alabama, 4, 19, 35-37

Alimony (see Spousal support)

Alternatives to divorce (see Reconciliation, Separation)

American Bar Association (ABA)
Family law section, 8

Annulment
definition of, 21
difference from divorce, 21-22
grounds for, 22-23
process, 22
contested, 22
defenses against granting, 23
status of children, 23
differences in state laws, 23

Application for entry of default, 72

Arbitration (see Mediation)

Arizona, 4, 19, 27, 35

Arizona child support guidelines, 57-59

Arkansas, 47, 53

Assault and battery, 3

Assets (see Marital assets)

Asset check, 60-61 (also see Collecting child support)

Attorney (see Legal representation)

B

Bankcard Holders of America, 105

Bankruptcy of spouse, 30

Battered spouse, 11 (also see Domestic violence)

Battered women's shelters, 9 (also see Domestic violence)

Bodily Harm, 8 (also see Domestic violence)

C

California, 27, 35

Certified Public Accountant (CPA) (see Accountant)

Child abuse (see Domestic violence, Custody, Child support, Visitation)

Child support
as part of divorce agreement, 3, 16, 20-21, 25
Arizona child support guidelines, 57-59
joint custody, 52
modifications to agreement, 57, 60
obligation of nonworking parent, 56
rights and responsibilities of parents, 3, 48, 73
special circumstances, 57

109

D